The Lamb is a touching and inspiring story that is sure to bring families closer to each other and the Lord.
—Steven Morris, Youth Minister

THE
LAMB

THE
LAMB

KEVIN ATCHLEY

Dedication

Every day we're given the opportunity to become greater people than we were the day before. This drive comes from a power we cannot comprehend. This book is dedicated to Jesus Christ, who makes it all possible.

However, as it was written:
"No eye has seen, no ear has heard, no mind has conceived, what God has prepared for those who love him."

1 Corinthians 2: 9

Acknowledgments

I wish I could better express how each person involved inspired and prompted me with this story and give credit where credit is due. Words cannot describe the feelings:

My parents' help and suggestions; my wife's unfailing belief; my children, who cheered me on.

My wife's family for their help and support;

My friends, brothers, and sisters, who gladly helped me and supported this endeavor with no thought of time or labor;

Charles and Janice Wood, for smiles, tears, and a thorough, analytical view of the project;

Steven Morris, an upcoming superstar in evangelism, whose name you will hear again, and his wife, Kimberly, for their kindness and input after countless phone calls and never once letting me know I was getting on their nerves;

Lucy Jones and her sister, Patricia Stewart, who in a short time had me more proficient than I ever was in junior English;

Rex and Amy Dollar, for sharing it with Addie and David.

Austin Emory, Lisa Goodvoice, Phillip and Anne Hatley, Laurie Loyd, Nic Richardson and last but not least, all the wonderful, kind, solid people at CreateSpace.

This story is a direct reflection of your kindness, belief, and generosity. Thank you.

Special thanks to EJ Barbee for drawing the pictures in this book.

Introduction

The main goal of this story is to glorify God. I hope it's not a stumbling block to those who may consider this work to have "added to or taken away" from the historical truths found in the Bible or those who struggle with relevancy issues typical of fictional stories.

I believe the Bible does not contain the Word of God; the Bible *is* the Word of God. There is no substitute. There are no alternatives. It is my hope that this story will edify everyone and help all to better realize the good news:

Jesus Christ lived as a man.

He was crucified on a cross.

He was resurrected on the third day.

Because of this sacrifice, we are made whole in the eyes of God and given the opportunity to enjoy a close, personal relationship with the creator of the universe.

Please accept this opportunity. Look into the Scriptures. See for yourself how easily and completely the Bible explains everything from the simplest questions of this short life to the plan of salvation for eternity.

—Kevin

CHAPTER ONE

I "t's not fair!" Steven shouted. "Why should I be responsible for caring about Judi when he gets to act however he wants, whenever he wants, to whoever he wants?" Steven's left eye was a deep, almost black, purple.

"Easy, Steven," his father said, hurrying around the house, anxiously looking for a scroll he was to deliver to the temple that morning.

"Steven, you know we try to be fair to all people," said his mother as she was busy preparing breakfast with her sister, May, whom they stayed with when they were in Jerusalem.

"Where did I put that scroll I was reading, Martha?" Steven's father shouted from another room.

"Fair! Is this fair?" Steven protested, pointing to his swollen eye.

"You were reading it last night, dear!" Steven's mother called to his father and then turned her attention back to him. "No, it's not fair. But think of Judi. His mother died, and he never sees his father. Is that fair?"

"But it's not by the bed. Didn't I bring it to bed?"

"I can't help it if his father spends all his time with those other priests making up those impossible laws."

"I'm not sure, dear. But is it fair?"

"Is it in the kitchen?"

"No, but I'm fair. That's all I want is fair. An eye for an eye. That's fair, isn't it? That's what they teach. That's what we learn, isn't it?" Steven argued.

"No, dear. It's not in the kitchen. Yes, that's what they teach, but what does that accomplish?"

"Is it in the dining room?"

"Yep, an eye for an eye. That's what I want. I want Judi's eye."

"Oh, Steven!"

"May, have you seen that scroll?"

"I think I'll take his right eye."

"Steven, stop!"

"Is it in the hall?"

"I'll take his right eye, and I'll throw it over the wall to the dogs."

"Steven, quiet!" his mother said in what was, for her, a most definite tone of voice.

"Here it is! Right by the door so I wouldn't forget it."

At that moment, time stood still as the three formed a triangle facing each other over the span of the house. Steven's jaws were clenched tight, and the glazed slant in his eyes showed his thoughts were a million miles away. Steven's mother's eyebrows were pulled together in a cross between concern and fear at what she had heard from her nine-year-old child. Steven's father stood by the door, beaming, with the lost scroll held out firmly in his hands.

After a long silence, Steven's mother was the first to speak. "You heard what Jesus said. We are to love our enemies. Pray for those who persecute you."[1]

Again they looked at each other. Looks of compassion were on the faces of both adults, but Steven's jaws seemed to clench just a little harder, and his eyes became a little more glaring as he stared at the floor and walked toward the door. Reaching the door, Steven turned to his parents and said, "It's just not fair. Why call them enemies if you're supposed to love them?"

At this, Steven turned and walked out the door. His parents looked at each other, understanding the pain he was feeling.

Steven's father stepped out of the door behind him. "Steven!" his father called. Steven stopped and turned with his eyes toward the ground. His father approached and put his arms around him. Pulling Steven close he said, "Don't forget about being in control of yourself. Don't let others dictate your actions. Whatever you choose in life, you have to have control to make it work." Steven's father handed him several small wrapped packages of food his mother and aunt had been working on.

"I know. Control. Gotta stay in control." Steven took the packages, turned, and again started down the street with his eyes glued to the ground.

"Don't forget, we're heading back to Capernaum after lunch," his father said.

A moment later he heard him shout, "We love you!"

Steven walked down the street like he had a thousand times before. Staring at the ground, he worked his way up to the main streets that led through Jerusalem. "It's just not fair," he mumbled. "Why should I care about someone like Judi?"

Steven walked through the streets of Jerusalem noticing no one. He skirted the temple and walked toward the
pool of Bethesda. Ahead, by the pool, he could see one of
his close friends, Maundi. He was one of the few people
Steven could talk to. He visited Maundi every day when he
was in Jerusalem. Maundi stayed by the pool of Bethesda.
His knees didn't work. He had never been able to get from
one place to another without crawling. There were people lying and standing all around the pool waiting for the
water to stir so they could quickly rush in and receive the
healing spirits.[2]

"Ah! If it's not Saint Steven. Right on time!" As Steven
knelt down, Maundi threw his arm around him as if preparing to have Steven help him into the pool. "Watch the
water now," he said, pausing. "Any minute it's going to stir,"
he said again with slow anticipation. "Come on now. Get
ready," he said with a caring, focused voice. "Here she goes.
Any second. I'll do a swan dive right in the middle!"

"Hush that over there! Nobody wants to hear that carrying on!" an old woman screeched from across the pool.
She had a very hunched back and was waiting by a pillar
on the other side of the pool. The woman repositioned herself with her back toward Steven and Maundi but where
she could still see the water.

"Never mind her," Maundi said, looking at Steven with
a smile. Maundi relaxed his eager position to jump into the
pool and rested on Steven with his arm around his shoulders. He stared back at the pool as if standing on the shores
of Galilee. "Someday we'll catch that water just right, and
in we'll go. Then no more broken knees!" Maundi's voice

KEVIN ATCHLEY

was energetic, almost happy. The way he had sounded every day for countless days in a row.

"Okay, Maundi. Any day now."

As Maundi lay back down on his mat with Steven's help, the reply he got was far from energetic, far from happy. "Uh oh!" Maundi grunted as he used his arms to position himself facing the pool. "Just a little faith, Steven." Maundi chuckled as he dreamingly gazed at the pool. Quickly turning his full attention back to Steven, Maundi reached out and grabbed Steven's ankle. "But what's got the most philosophical philosopher in all of Jerusalem so far down in the dumps this fine morning?"

Steven sat down beside Maundi and handed him one of the wrapped parcels of food. "It's just not fair," Steven said, almost sounding tired.

"Oh, there's no guarantees," said Maundi. "You never know what kind of curves life's going to throw you."

"I know there's no guarantees, but why can't things be like they used to? I want an eye!"

"Ah ha!" Maundi cackled with a high-pitched laugh. "An eye for an eye, huh?"

"Yeah! I might take both eyes! I might take his whole head!"

Maundi's cheerful expression completely vanished. Still gazing at the pool, Maundi sighed. "That's what it leads to, Steven."

"It worked for hundreds of years, didn't it?" Steven asked.

Looking back at Steven, Maundi mumbled, "The Law. Hundreds of years it was, the Law. You knew what was going to happen, but there was no hope. I'm not sure if you can call that working."

It was almost silent around the pool. Everyone was extremely focused on the water, looking for any kind of activity. Steven and Maundi both looked over at the woman across the pool, who had changed the position in which she was standing.

"You can't fix every problem by getting even with somebody. Most of the time that makes you just like them. Listen to your father. He knows the Law points toward compassion."

"I know. But why does it have to be so hard?" Steven asked.

This brought a smile back to Maundi's face. "Not much good comes from the easy road, Steven. It's always give and take. There's always a sacrifice."

"Where is everybody?" Steven wondered out loud. Looking around, it suddenly dawned on him that the streets were not nearly as crowded as they normally were at this time in the morning.

"Find Jesus," Maundi said, turning to Steven. "Did you get to hear him yesterday?"

"No," Steven replied. "After Judi and his band of hooligans rolled me around in the street down at the northeast gate, I missed the last group that was going out to hear him."

"Oh, Steven. The hills in the east are always full of dogs. They live in all the small caves and under the ledges." Maundi's face was full of concern. "Don't go out there alone."

"I know. I know. You sound just like Mom," Steven said.

"It's the truth, Steven. You've got to watch out for the dogs."

"I know. I know. Beware of the dogs. Maundi, what do you think is going on? Where is everybody?"

"I heard earlier from one of the traders that they saw him heading toward Jerusalem early this morning." The smile had returned once again to Maundi's face. At this news, Steven jumped to his feet with a smile of anticipation and excitement himself.

"Jesus? When? What time? Which gate were they heading toward?" The memories of what happened the day before completely vanished from Steven's mind. Scooping up the small packages of food, Steven hurriedly handed them in Maundi's direction. "Here. Here! I'll be back. Um, give one to Rachel when she comes, and, uh, you keep one, and…" Steven had turned at this point and was headed down the street. He turned back to Maundi and shouted as he ran backward, "Give one to Azack and the widow Mireb!"

Maundi waved to Steven. "Don't you worry. I'll take care of things. Hey, if you find Jesus, send him my way. I've got a little favor to ask him!" Steven had turned and was now in a full run up the hill toward the temple.

"I will!" he shouted back. "I will!"

CHAPTER TWO

S teven was a master at making his way through the city. He was equally good at working his way through a crowd of people. It didn't matter what kind of celebration or how crowded the streets were, Steven was still the fastest at getting from one place to another. He moved like the wind. He was up and down, in and out, and over and under. Steven raced through the streets, which were still rather empty. As he neared the temple, people were gathering at corners, and Steven could hear them murmuring. "It was him. We saw him. He's going to the temple." This fueled Steven's anticipation, and he ran even faster.

As Steven got closer, he turned down a narrow alley he always used as a shortcut to get into the temple area. Steven knew this part of Jerusalem best from spending time with his father. This was also the place where Steven listened and talked to so many people about things that he found so interesting.

Steven was near the temple walls, running full speed, when from nowhere a rope was pulled tight across the alleyway. Not seeing the rope, he tripped, falling hard onto the dusty street. Steven threw out his arms but rolled and came to a grinding stop on his right cheek.

From the corners and in between the little buildings along the alley where the rope had been pulled poured laughing boys that were about the same age as Steven.

Laughing and pointing, they walked toward the middle of the street where Steven was slowly pushing himself up.

One boy, whom the others seemed to center around, wasn't laughing. He wasn't even smiling. "You're slipping, Steven. I had a feeling you'd be heading this way this morning. Quite a crowd in the temple. On your way to see the magic show?" The other boys laughed even louder as they hit shoulders and pointed at Steven standing and dusting himself off. The boys became absolutely silent as Steven walked toward the boy in the middle, who still had no expression on his face at all. Steven stared at the boy as he approached him and stood face-to-face. Both boys were clenching their fists.

"That was good, Judi. I never saw it coming. And I'd love to stay and chat, but I think I'd have more intelligent conversation with the dogs in the east hills." Steven's eyes were slanted, glaring right through Judi, who was standing just inches from him.

Suddenly Steven's eyes widened, which surprised Judi. "Besides, he's here today! Jesus is in the temple!" Steven said with excitement. Steven backed away from Judi and was looking for a way of escape as the other boys began to circle around him.

"Why do you spend your time with those losers?" Judi snapped sharply. "Everyone knows he's just a joke. He's just a wannabe putting on a show. A wannabe like your messenger-boy father."

While Judi was talking, Steven continued looking around for a way out. Steven suddenly jumped up and grabbed the porch of one of the buildings beside the alley.

He swung his feet up and over and stood on the roof above the other boys. He jumped to the building, ran down the top of the wall, and then jumped to the steps leading to one of the back rooms of the temple.

As Steven disappeared into the temple, he could hear the boys shouting, and Judi yelling, "Another day, Steven! Another day!" Steven hurried through the passageways toward the center of the temple.

Chapter Three

Steven wound through the dark passageways in the outskirts of the temple that made their way to the temple courts. Steven had run through these hallways a thousand times; so, he ran thinking of only one thing: seeing and hearing Jesus.

Racing down the last set of steps to the courtyard, Steven saw the crowd circled around the court as they usually were, but the sounds he heard were far from usual.

Coming in from the back of the courtyard, Steven ran by the altars, worked his way through a small group of people, and stood by the cages of animals that were being kept for sacrificial offerings.

What Steven saw was the farthest thing from his imagination. As soon as he reached the front of the crowd, a table that had been thrown not far from the center of the yard landed on the ground. As the table crashed into pieces, coins scattered and jingled across the stone courtyard.

Then he saw him. The man he had only heard in calm, reverent settings speaking about faith, hope, and love was standing in the center of the courtyard bare-chested, letting doves escape from their cages. He then grabbed a nearby table and hurled it through the air. He opened the stalls that caged the calves and rams and ran them out of the courtyard with a whip he made from cords of the temple curtains. He then turned to the group of merchants and religious leaders who were standing amazed, their eyes as big as saucers. He stood with an open stance. His muscular arms were at his sides holding the whip. There was fire in his eyes, and he breathed heavily as he shouted to the crowd, "Get these out of here! How dare you turn my Father's house into a market?"

Animals that had been freed from their cages ran wildly through the courtyard and escaped through the crowd of people out of the temple. Steven listened to Jesus shout to the merchants and religious leaders about turning the temple into a den of thieves when he felt something tug on his shirt sleeve. It may have happened more than once, but Steven didn't notice in the excitement of what was happening.

Steven looked down to find a pristine lamb with its head through the bars of a cage pulling on his sleeve. Steven looked around. Everyone was very focused on Jesus, who was straightening his clothes as he continued talking. Steven looked back at the lamb that was still looking up at him with big eyes, batting his long eyelashes. Steven looked at the crowd of people as he slowly pulled the pin on the lamb's cage. When the pin was free, the latch fell, and the cage door swung open. The lamb ran from the cage right up to Steven and jumped into his arms.

The crowd in the entire temple was absolutely silent. Steven and the lamb stood watching Jesus as he prepared to leave the temple. Steven heard the religious leaders shouting to Jesus, "What gives you the authority to do this? You could be arrested. You could be whipped. Show us a sign!" Jesus was facing the front of the temple, and the crowd parted without a sound to let him pass.

Jesus stopped before starting down the temple steps. Turning around, he looked back at Steven and the lamb. Jesus's head lowered as he looked right into Steven's eyes. He nodded, and Steven saw a smile form on the corners of Jesus's mouth and in his eyes. Jesus turned to the religious leaders and said, "Destroy this temple, and I will raise it again in three days." He then quickly turned and walked through the crowd and out of the temple.[3]

Steven wasn't sure what he felt. His whole body tingled, and he felt like he was floating. He stared at the crowd, not seeing anything at all. Steven came to his senses when he felt the lamb struggling to get down from his arms. Steven set the lamb on the ground and then looked back at the crowd. Some were smiling, and some were scurrying around trying to catch freed animals. One of the religious leaders was shouting, "Get those animals back in here! Lock the cages! Pick up that money!"

Steven saw Judi run through the courtyard to the man who was shouting. "Dad! What happened?"

The man did not even look at Judi. "Get that one! Bring it over here! Not now, Judi. Bag up the money!" Judi stood back as his father continued shouting commands. He approached his father a second time. "Father, what can I do?" Judi asked.

His father glared down at him and yelled, "Not now, Judi! I don't have time!" Steven recognized the same emotionless stare on Judi's face he had seen in the alley earlier.

His father turned to the other religious leaders, "Everyone to the Great Hall. This Jesus has gone too far this time."

CHAPTER FOUR

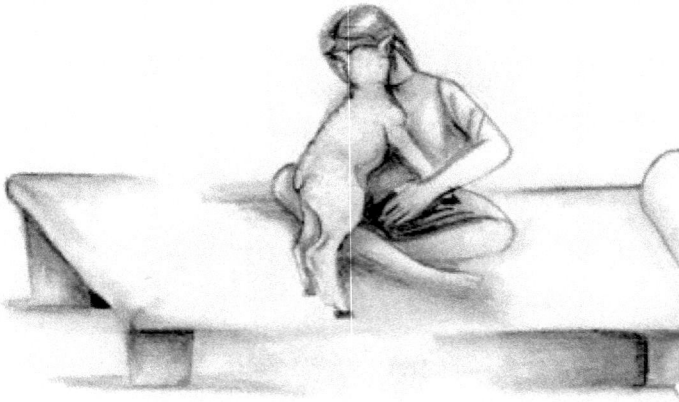

Steven ran through a side exit of the temple court that led to the street. The lamb was right behind him. Steven was overjoyed with the idea of having this new friend. Most of Steven's friends were older people his family took care of. All of them had some kind of physical ailment that kept them from being able to care for themselves. Steven's family, along with some of his aunts and uncles, made sure these people had food and shelter when it was necessary. Steven didn't get along well with children his own age. It seemed no one was interested in finding the truth. Everyone was satisfied just following along, never questioning "what if?" "What if" there was more to it all?

Until Jesus! Steven just had to talk to him. There were so many questions to ask, so many people to tell him about. Steven could never find the right moment to approach him though. Jesus was so busy. He was continually surrounded. Today's eye contact in the temple was the closest they had come to words. And that was enough. Steven had an overwhelming sense that everything was okay. Nothing could get him down now.

Steven ran from the temple with the lamb close behind. He took every shortcut he knew to distance himself from the temple as fast as he could. He ran straight back to his aunt's house and came crashing through the door, slamming it shut behind him and his new friend.

"My!" his mother exclaimed. "What could possibly be after you? Wait a minute. What do we have here?" Steven's mother and aunt moved toward Steven and the lamb, smiling and doting as if they were seeing a new baby for the first time. "Isn't he precious? Oh, he's just adorable. Beautiful!" The two women cooed as they knelt down and hugged the lamb toward them.

Shaking his head, Steven smiled smugly, immediately feeling the pain in his cheek. Wincing, he again felt the pain of his swollen left eye. Noticing Steven's pain, his mother turned her attention from the lamb to him. "Steven, what happened to you? Where did you get this lamb? Why are your clothes so dirty? Steven, what happened?"

Steven was so excited and elated with his encounter with Jesus at the temple and his newfound friend, he could hardly explain to his mother and aunt what had happened. "I talked to Jesus!"

"You talked to Jesus?" Steven's mother and aunt said simultaneously.

"Well, he looked at me. And a table crashed, and money went all over!"

"Whoa, Steven. Slow down," his mother urged, a smile of bewilderment on her face.

"There were animals running all over the place! The lamb pulled on my sleeve! He looked me right in the eye!"

"Steven!" cried his mother as his aunt went to the kitchen, laughing. "Slow down. Come into the kitchen, and tell us everything that happened."

Steven proceeded to tell his mother and aunt all that had happened at the temple earlier that morning. His mother sat listening quietly with a look of concern growing on her face. As Steven was ending his story, his mother replied, "But, Steven, this isn't your lamb."

Martha had no more finished her statement when Steven's father came barreling through the door just as Steven had earlier. "You won't believe what happened at the temple this morning!" Isa's exclamation was cut short by the look of concern and frustration on the faces of the three people sitting in the kitchen. "Or maybe you will. What is it? What's wrong?" Steven's father asked.

As he approached the three, the lamb popped its head around Steven's chair and looked at Steven's father. "Well, hello there. Where did you come from?"

"He's mine!" Steven shrieked. "I got him! He let all the animals go. He's supposed to be mine! He told me I could have him!"

"You talked to Jesus?" Steven's father asked with a wave of excitement, both at the idea of speaking to Jesus and the hope of answering the questionable possession of the lamb. "I guess you did hear what happened," Isa said.

"Well, he didn't actually talk to me. But he looked at me and said everything was okay."

"How can you look at someone and say everything is okay?" asked his mother.

"I don't know!" Steven cried in exasperation. "But he did." Steven's mother and father exchanged worried looks as the lamb cowered behind Steven. "Don't you say everything happens for a reason?" Steven asked his parents.

"Well, yes," his mother began to reply as Steven interrupted and fired another argument.

"Look at him. I saved his life." The lamb crept out from behind Steven and struck a prominent, majestic pose, batting its big eyes at the onlookers. "There must be a reason. There must be," Steven said as he reached out and stroked the lamb.

Steven's parents were again exchanging looks of concern. "Why don't you really ask him?" The comment made by his aunt floated in the kitchen. Steven and his parents turned to her, and she repeated the question, "Why don't you really ask Jesus?"

"What do you mean, May?" Martha replied.

"Ask him. Ask him if it's okay to keep the lamb."

Steven's mother looked at his father, who had an uncertain look on his face.

"I will!" Steven shouted. "I'll ask him. I'm sure he'll remember. Maybe we'll see him on the way to Capernaum today!" Steven was alive again with this new plan of hope. He scooped the lamb off the floor and headed to the back of the house to ready his things for the trip.

The look of concern still hung heavily on the faces of Steven's parents.

"What if he says no?" Isa asked.

"What if he says yes?" Martha replied. "Is the lamb Jesus's to give away?"

Steven's aunt interjected with a smile. "If Jesus is who we hope he is, everything belongs to him. It won't hurt Steven to search for this answer anyway."

Steven's father raised his eyebrows as Martha replied, "It depends on where he goes searching. And Jesus' lamb or not, that is definitely Caiaphas's temple," she said, stressing the name of the high priest. "He won't take someone letting his animals go or scattering his money lightly."

"No," Isa replied. "I'm supposed to leave with word to Capernaum at once." The three adults stared blankly at the table, fearing the possible consequences for Jesus.

Steven sat on his bed holding the lamb, which beamed up at him. "I'll never let them have you," he said to the lamb. "I'll run away first. I'll go far, far away, and they'll never find us." The lamb leaned its head up and rubbed its face against Steven's cheek. The soft touch of the lamb's fleece felt good to Steven, even against the scratches and bruises.

CHAPTER FIVE

The road between Jerusalem and Capernaum was busy. There were always people going from one place to another. Most people were walking, but a few were in carts, chariots, or riding horses. There were traders, soldiers, travelers, and everyone was in a group. Never did a person walk along the roads by themselves. This was because of the dogs. Steven had never really even seen the dogs, up close anyway. He had heard stories, though. Since he was a child, Steven had been told stories of the dogs that roamed the hills, catching the lone traveler unaware.

Steven and his parents were on a nice wagon owned by the synagogue in Capernaum. His father took the wagon when he was delivering different scrolls and manuscripts. If he was just delivering messages, he rode a horse. Steven and his mother often rode with him when he was delivering items in the cart. Steven traveled with his father every chance he got. He had made the trip between Capernaum and Jerusalem more times than he could ever possibly remember, but never had a trip back to Capernaum been so enjoyable and so full of excitement. Steven and the lamb rode in the back of the cart. He was sure every person they passed noticed him and his new friend. As he lay back on a pile of bags and blankets, the warm sun shone on his face. Steven hadn't felt this good in a long time.

There were many sounds heard along the road. Sometimes Steven heard laughing and singing. People talked and visited within their group. Sometimes he heard crying. They were traveling along the Jordan River at Aenon near Salim when Steven heard men arguing in the distance. As they approached a stretch of road next to the river, it became evident one man was arguing with three other men. Steven's father brought the cart to a stop because of the people in the road crowded around listening to the shouting match. Suddenly, for no apparent reason, the men stopped their arguing and turned toward the river. As the crowd separated, a wild-looking man appeared from the edge of the water.

His hair was long and untamed, as was his beard. He wore a rough, brown robe with a leather belt unlike the traditional colored clothes most everyone else wore. As he approached the men, it would have seemed completely natural for someone who looked like him to scream and attack the men, but he said nothing at all.

Steven's mother whispered to his father, "It's John the Baptist."

Steven had seen John the Baptist before, and just like the few previous times, his appearance was just as breathtaking. Steven had heard him speak on different occasions while traveling with his father. The absolute certainty with which he spoke, combined with his appearance, was most captivating.

Finally, one of the three who was arguing with the man said, "Rabbi, that man who was with you on the other side of the Jordan—the one you witnessed about—well, he is baptizing, and everyone is going to him."

To this the man replied, "A man can receive only what is given him from heaven. You yourselves can testify that I said, 'I am not the Christ but am sent ahead of him.' The bride belongs to the bridegroom. The friend who attends the bridegroom waits and listens for him and is full of joy when he hears the bridegroom's voice. That joy is mine, and it is now complete. He must become greater. I must become less."[4] When John had finished speaking these words, it was as if he had dismissed the crowd. Everyone left silently as the crowd disbursed.

"Who's getting married?" Steven asked.

"No one's getting married, Steven," his father said. "The bride is the main attraction. The bridegroom gets the attention because it's their day. John compared himself to the one who attends the bridegroom."

"What does that have to do with getting married?" Steven asked again.

"Well, nothing with getting married," his father answered with a chuckle. "It appears John was talking about whom people should listen to, who should get people's attention. Like the bridegroom on his wedding day."

"After the incident at the temple, I'm afraid Jesus is going to be getting a lot of attention," his mother added.

The crowd had broken enough that Steven and his parents could begin making their way on to Capernaum. With the lamb lying across his chest, Steven settled back on the blankets and drifted into a deep sleep. He fell asleep imagining talking with Jesus. The scene at the temple, the smile, and the nod he got from Jesus were etched in his mind. As the wagon rocked slowly down the road, Steven slept with a smile on his face. He felt safe, calm, and in control.

CHAPTER SIX

S teven was glad to be back in Capernaum. He loved going with his father and seeing his friends in different cities, but he was always glad to be home. Especially this time. Steven seldom slept in late, and today was no different; he was up at the crack of dawn. Steven immediately recognized the wonderful smell of bread and knew his mother was making her delicious loaves. His father, still in his bed clothes, was in the kitchen with his mother. Steven and the lamb both came sliding into the kitchen as Steven looked for the small parcels of food that were always ready for him to deliver.

"Whoa there, partner! What's the big hurry this morning?" his father asked.

"I gotta go!" he answered excitedly. "I can't wait to show my lamb to Valmus and Sera and Margaret. I hope Sera's feeling better."

"I heard from her mother she's worse. She can't even get out of bed," replied Steven's mother. "It's a shame to see such a sweet little girl sick for so long."

"Maybe I can take my lamb by her house to see her?" Steven said.

"Maybe so," his father agreed. "That would surely make her feel better."

"You haven't forgotten your agreement, have you?" Steven's mother quizzed him. "You were going to find Jesus and ask him about *your* lamb," she said, stressing the your. The expression on Steven's face sunk.

"It's okay, Steven," his father said encouragingly. "It'll be a great experience."

"What if he says no?" Steven asked, looking at the floor. "What if he says he's not mine and I shouldn't keep him?"

"Don't worry," his father said. "There are reasons for everything. Search for the reasons. Talk to God. He'll guide you."

Steven paused in thought for a moment and then revived with excitement looking at the lamb, which rubbed his head on Steven's leg. "I will. I'll find him. I'm sure he wants me to keep him. There's got to be a great reason!" Steven exclaimed.

Steven snatched the wrap containing the food and ran into the crisp morning air. People were just beginning to move around the city, and Steven heard roosters from several different locations. The sky still had a hint of morning red as Steven made his way to his first stop.

"One of those is yours!" he heard his mother shout as he headed toward the south gate.

Valmus was always at the main entrance of the city first thing in the morning. He took handouts from morning traffic and then moved to the synagogue, which was not far away, when it got too warm. There were not many people coming into the city yet, and Valmus stood alone at the side of the road.

"Valmus! Look here!" Steven cried.

Valmus looked up in surprise at the call. "Ah, Steven, ole' buddy. How are you? Did you get back last night?" the man replied.

Valmus reached out his left hand and embraced Steven as he ran up to him. Valmus's right hand remained at his side. It was completely immobile. From birth, his right arm was bent at his elbow, and his forearm and hand had never developed into more than a withered piece of flesh and bone.

"What's this? Have you taken up shepherding? A man after King David's own heart," Valmus said, recognizing the lamb.

"I got him in Jerusalem. I saw Jesus. It was at the temple. He talked to me—well, kind of…sort of." As usual, Steven found his thoughts and words rolling into a jumbled mess when he got excited. Valmus smiled.

"I heard there was some rat killing going on at the temple in Jerusalem." Valmus kept up on all the latest news from talking with the people he met coming into the city from different places. "It appears Jesus is making quite a name for himself, going toe to toe with Caiaphas."

"It was awesome. I saw the whole thing," Steven exclaimed. "He told them the temple was not a store. He called it 'his Father's house' and said that wasn't what it was supposed to be used for." Steven had regained his composure and was fishing around in the wrap for the food to give to Valmus.

"Listen to Jesus," Valmus said. "I really believe he has come to show us just what we're supposed to do." He accepted the parcel from Steven with a smile. "I'm not sure what that is yet, but I believe he's the one to tell us."

Steven looked at Valmus, whose expression had turned to a frown. "What is it, Valmus?" Steven asked.

Valmus slowly replied in a sad voice, "I overheard the religious leaders at the synagogue. They were all happy because King Herod had John the Baptist arrested and put into jail."[5]

"In jail? But we saw him yesterday! At Aenon near Salim! He was talking to some men about Jesus. He was the guy who attended the bridegroom, and Jesus was supposed to get all the attention because it was his day."

"I'm not sure about all of that, Steven," Valmus said. "Apparently the soldiers took him to Jerusalem last night."

"I can't believe it. We just saw him," Steven replied in wonder.

"I know. I've never seen him or heard him speak, but what I have heard about him was he kept to himself. If he had something to say to someone, he told them. And he never lied. It was never for personal gain, like some I know in the synagogues," Valmus said and immediately smiled. "Enough sad talk, though. What do you and your new friend have planned for today?"

"I've got a few more people to see this morning. Have you seen Margaret? I'm going to Sera's house, and then I'm going to find Jesus," Steven answered in a bold and determined voice.

"Well, you've got a busy day ahead of you. Margaret is probably at the well. I haven't heard where Jesus is. I will, though. A lot of people are talking about him," Valmus said. "Check with me later at the synagogue, and maybe I'll have heard where he is."

"All right. I'm going to show my lamb to Sera and then find Margaret. I'll see you at the synagogue."

Valmus cupped his hand behind Steven's neck. "Thank you, Steven. And tell your folks thank you, too."

"I will," Steven replied as he turned, and he and the lamb started back toward the heart of the city.

CHAPTER SEVEN

The city was beginning to wake up. The streets were becoming alive with people setting up their goods for sale. As Steven and the lamb made their way back into the city, he stopped to notice the familiar sounds and smells of home. He smiled at the lamb, which jumped ahead as if he anticipated exploring this new place. One last rooster crowed as morning seemed to just disappear.

As Steven and the lamb worked their way through the bustling streets, he noticed the smiles of people admiring his new friend. This gave Steven a warm feeling of importance and belonging. Steven found the lamb was just as quick working through the crowds as he was. He would dart out ahead but look back to make sure he was going in the right direction. They made their way to the northeast side of the city to nicer homes that belonged to many of the leaders and rulers. The houses were built into the hillside overlooking the sea. They had fine white sides of stone and red tile roofs.

Sera's house had a huge palm tree in the front with flowers planted around its base. Two large urns were on either side of the entrance leading into the yard. Crawling up the wall from the urns were variegated vines covered with clusters of violet blossoms. Steven and the lamb walked the short path to the front door, which was made from thick timbers. Even though he had been to Sera's house countless times, Steven felt a familiar uneasy feeling as he banged the metal knocker, which echoed throughout the entire house.

Steven heard the latch click, and the heavy door slowly creaked open. In the doorway appeared a smiling woman, and the butterflies in Steven's stomach disappeared. "Good morning, Rosetta," Steven said, smiling.

"Well, good morning, Steven, and friend. What a fine pair of callers we have this beautiful morning," replied the woman.

"Isn't he beautiful? And smart too. I got him in Jerusalem. I talked to Jesus."

"You talked to Jesus?" Rosetta immediately questioned.

"Well, sort of." Steven found the means to stifle his excitement. "It's kind of a long story."

"I see." The woman smiled. "It sounds like quite the adventure. I bet you've come to see Miss Sera?" Rosetta asked, stepping inside the house to allow Steven and the lamb to enter.

"Yes," Steven replied. "I heard she was feeling worse, and I hoped seeing my lamb would make her feel better."

"I'm sure. I'm sure," Rosetta answered and continued with a voice of despair. "Miss Sera is certainly not improving as we'd like, and the doctors don't seem to know what's wrong." There was a crack in Rosetta's voice like she was going to cry. Steven was looking at the floor when Rosetta stepped in front of him and gently took hold of both his shoulders. The concerned look on her face had relaxed, and she was smiling again as she said, "But with faith, hope, and love, anything can happen. And you, sir, have all three."

She started talking in almost a whisper as she led Steven to the interior of the house toward the stairs. "Now we won't be able to stay long, but a short visit is sure to lift Miss Sera's spirits. The room is kept dim so she can rest easier. Talk softly. No sudden movements or loud noises." Rosetta and the two guests arrived to an upstairs room with the door barely open.

Rosetta pushed the door open an inch or two more, and the three squeezed into the room. The room was dimly lit indeed. Thin beams of light hung in the air, which came through the shutters that covered the window. Before Steven's eyes adjusted to the light, he heard a terribly frail voice come from the corner of the room. "Rosetta?" As Rosetta started toward the voice, Steven slowly made out the shape of a bed with a tiny person lying under a sheet.

"Yes, dear?" he heard Rosetta say.

Steven began to walk toward the bed but felt like he was somewhere else. He gained his senses when the lamb nudged him closer to the bed.

"You have some guests to see you, Miss Sera. Steven's here, and he brought a friend."

Steven's eyes had adjusted to the light, but he was having trouble adjusting to the dark, dreary conditions of the room. "Hi, Sera," he finally was able to say. "How...how are you doing?"

"Hello, Steven. Come closer."

Rosetta stepped to the side and put her hand on Steven's shoulder as he moved closer to the bed. "I'm sorry to see you're not feeling better."

"It's okay, Steven. I'll be better soon. What have you been up to? Have you been anywhere with your father?"

Steven felt his uneasiness disappear as he sat on the edge of the bed. Sera tried to sit up but settled back to the bed and rested her head on the pillow. Steven felt his excitement grow as he took Sera by the hand and began telling his friend about Jerusalem.

Rosetta interrupted, "Now you two enjoy your visit, but it will have to be short. Sera must stay calm and rested."

"Okay, Rosetta. I'll only stay a minute."

"Thank you, Steven," Rosetta said as she turned and left the room.

The time passed quickly. The lamb had made its way into Steven's lap, and Sera rubbed its head. The lamb pushed back against her hand and then nibbled at her fingers. Steven told Sera about Jerusalem, seeing Jesus, and getting the lamb. They were talking about Steven's plans for finding Jesus in the country east of the sea when Rosetta entered the room. Rosetta patted the lamb and couldn't help smiling. It had been a while since she had seen Sera—whose beautiful smile was plainly seen in the dimly lit room—so happy.

"Steven, remember when we used to play in the rocks down by the beach?" Sera asked.

"Yes, Sera. That was always so much fun."

"I want to do that again," she said faintly.

"We will," Steven said. "Soon."

"Very soon," Rosetta repeated as she stroked the young girl's head. "You rest now, and Steven and his friend will call again."

Sera turned her face away as if already asleep. "Good-bye, Steven," she said in the faintest of voices. A slight smile could still be made out on her face.

Steven and Rosetta walked to the front door without saying a word. "Thank you for coming to visit, Steven," Rosetta finally said. "Lord Jairus and my lady will be so happy you called."

Steven was looking at the floor. "I had no idea she was feeling that bad."

"The doctors come every day, but no one has been able to help her." Rosetta sounded like she was going to cry again.

"I know someone who can help her! Jesus! Jesus can help Sera." Steven said brightly. "And I'm going to find him. Goodbye, Rosetta!" Steven called as he and the lamb darted out the open door back toward the bustling city.

CHAPTER EIGHT

By now, Capernaum was in full swing. The sun was warm, and the city was filled with all the familiar sounds and smells that made Steven feel at home. Steven felt extra special this morning, though. He was filled with a feeling of undeniable confidence and determination as he and the lamb worked through the streets like the wind.

The main street leading to the synagogue was filled with merchants. They had everything he could possibly imagine. There were pots and pans, spices, chickens, produce, and foods of all kinds. Margaret carried water from the well and set up a booth close to the steps of the synagogue. "Good morning, Margaret!" Steven exclaimed as he approached her brightly covered tent.

"Oh! Good morning, Steven," she replied in a tired voice. Margaret had a large jar of water with a dipper in it set on a bench. She had clay bowls for people to drink from as they came and went from the synagogue. Margaret was middle aged but looked and sounded very old. "It's good to have you home, Steven." Margaret was sitting on a bundle of blankets leaning on the bench with one arm. "And who is this with you?" she said wearily, noticing the lamb.

"Isn't he beautiful?" Steven replied, not even thinking of the whole story. "I'm sorry you don't feel well, Margaret," he said, handing her a small parcel of food. "Is there anything I can get for you?"

"Oh, Steven," said the woman as she hung her head. "You do so much as it is. If it wasn't for you and your parents, I wouldn't be here."

"You'll feel better soon, Margaret," Steven said.

"That's for sure. Nothing lasts forever, but twelve years seems like a very long time," she said with a faint smile.

"Have you seen Valmus?" asked Steven. "I'm supposed to meet him here. I'm going to find Jesus. He can do amazing things. He gave me this lamb—well, sort of. He can help you too, Margaret." Steven's look of concern changed to excitement as Margaret smiled. "He can help us all!" he exclaimed.

"I've heard great things about this Jesus," Margaret replied. "You're just the man to talk to him too," she said. Steven's expression went back to concern as he looked down. "Valmus is up at the top of the steps by the pillars in the shade," Margaret said as she brushed Steven's hair away from his eyes. "Don't worry. You're a very special boy, Steven. You'll find Jesus."

"I will," Steven said, smiling, though still looking down. "I'll find him.

Steven and the lamb started up the steps. He stopped and looked back at Margaret, "You rest, Margaret. I'll see you soon." The woman waved the arm she had been leaning on and settled back on the blankets without saying a word. Steven and the lamb turned and raced on to the top of the huge stone stairway.

The synagogue was a busy place as well, but Steven was no stranger to the formalities here. People were coming and going. There were people praying alone and in groups.

Many were resting in the shade of the huge pillars and overhang at the front of the synagogue. A man standing on a carved piece of stone was reading from a rolled manuscript, the kind Steven had seen so many times. He wondered if it might be one he and his family brought back from Jerusalem.

The top of the stairs offered an exhilarating view of the city. The street below, lined with palm trees, was a sea of people, colors, and animals. "For years I've been listening to them read from those scrolls." Steven heard a familiar voice say behind him. "Do you know what he's reading?" Valmus asked rather sadly.

"It sounds like Isaiah," Steven replied.

"Oh, what a bright boy," Valmus said with rising spirit as they both looked out at the city. "For years, they've read that someone is coming, someone special, a king no doubt. And now someone has appeared among the people who apparently can do things no person has ever done before. Great things. If the prophecies are true, the greatest thing Jesus offers is ours after we leave this world, but there's more."

"What is it, Valmus?" Steven asked.

Valmus smiled as he looked far away and then finally answered. "It's the hope he gives us while we're here," he replied.

"I hope I can find him. Have you heard where he is?" Steven asked.

Valmus turned to Steven and put his left hand on his shoulder. "I have," he replied. "People have come in and say he's left Jerusalem. After I saw you this morning, a woman came in the South Gate who had talked to Jesus at the well in Sychar near Mount Gerzim. She was very excited."

"Maybe he's coming here," Steven replied eagerly.

"Maybe so," Valmus said. "Be patient, and keep searching. You'll find him. Pray. That always helps."

"I will, Valmus," Steven said. Steven started down the steps when he heard Valmus call after him. "Steven, don't leave on your own. Be careful out there." Steven smiled and headed back down the stairs. "I will, Valmus. I will," he called back.

CHAPTER NINE

Steven woke early with his usual vigor and enthusiasm. As he stirred, the lamb jumped off the bed, and they headed to the larger part of the house. Steven heard familiar voices and smelled the wonderful smell coming from the kitchen as he raced behind the lamb.

"Good morning, Steven," he heard from several people as he and the lamb stood in the center of attention.

"What a beautiful animal," Steven heard a husky voice say.

"Uncle Simon!" Steven shouted, running to the man. "It's been so long!" Steven jumped into the bearded man's arms and hugged his neck.

"A beautiful little animal indeed," Simon said. "And what a lovely little lamb he has, too." Steven heard his mother and father laugh as Simon sat Steven back on the floor, kneeling beside him.

"Isn't he beautiful?" Steven asked. "Jesus gave him to me—well, sort of. I'm going to ask and make sure,"

"He's the man to talk to," Simon said.

Steven knew his uncle Simon was an excitable person, but this morning he noticed an unusual sense of urgency. "I was just telling your parents I've been with Jesus. Three weeks ago, Andrew and I were fishing, and he came to us. The things he said…and the way he said them. I've never met anyone like him."

"We had fished all night and caught nothing. Nothing! We were in the shallows starting to wash our nets, and Jesus called to us. He got into my boat and taught a group of people gathered on the shore. After he spoke Jesus told us to go back, to put our nets down, and try again. I was tired and didn't want to, but we did. You wouldn't believe all the fish. The nets tore there were so many![6] He's wonderful! So peaceful. So confident and sure of what he says. And the way he helps people. He's either teaching, preaching, or healing. It's amazing."

Steven was captivated by the way his uncle was speaking and the look in his eyes. He had heard him rave about things before, but it was about rough seas or the weather, not such miraculous things.

"Jesus says he's come with good news, that heaven has come, that God is with us and cares about us. Jesus says he can heal us—not just from physical sickness but from spiritual sickness too. He says there is no sin problem too big or too small for him to handle. Jesus speaks of a relationship with God, just the way Mom and Dad used to say, Martha," Simon said to Steven's mother. His arms were spread wide, and he had a look of amazement on his face.

"Simon, I'm so proud of you," Steven's mother replied, hugging him. "You've come such a long way."

"I don't quite understand it all yet," Simon said, "but I'm staying with him. James and John came, too. I really feel we're doing the right thing."

"What does Father say?" asked Steven's mother in her concerned voice.

"I talked to him and Zebedee. They're both happy. They both say we should do what we feel is right. Jesus is the answer. I'm sure. He only wants the best for everyone."

"I'm sure he wants me to keep this lamb," Steven stated proudly. "I know he wanted me to have this lamb. I could see it in his eyes."

"Then I'm sure he does," Simon replied. "Jesus seems particularly interested in helping those who try to help themselves. Not those who never accept help for anything, but those who try and believe. Like you, Steven." Steven smiled and looked at his parents. "You have to want Jesus's help and believe he can help you. Jesus told us he just came through Nazareth, his hometown, and they rejected him."

"No!" said Steven's father and mother. "I'm afraid for him," Steven's father said. "He has no fear in speaking right and wrong. The religious leaders are in a terrible uproar about how people listen and follow him."

"It's true. Thousands of people are following him, listening to the good news, and bringing their sick and suffering. It's absolutely wonderful," said Simon, scratching the lamb behind the ears. "You can find him, Steven. Follow the crowds, and don't leave the city alone," which was seconded by Steven's parents. "Jesus is always helping people. Like you and your folks," Simon said with a smile, mussing Steven's morning hair even more.

"We couldn't do it without you, Simon," Martha said, stepping forward and hugging him again. "You're a great brother."

"Yes, Simon," Isa said, squeezing the man's shoulder. "Thank you for the fish."

"Yes, yes," Simon said with a hearty laugh. "I must be off, though. I'm going to see Mother, and then I may be gone for a while." Simon said this smiling, his arms on Steven's parents' shoulders, who in turn had their arms on Steven's shoulders. It somewhat resembled a group hug, with the lamb right in the middle. Simon turned to walk away and then looked back at Steven. "You'll find him, Steven. I'm sure of it," he said.

"It might be today," Steven said. With this, they all exchanged smiles again, and Simon left.

"Steven," his mother said in that sneaky way she spoke when she wanted him to do something.

"Yes, Mother?" he replied, knowing what was coming.

"Why don't you help me salt these fish, and we'll make your parcels to deliver on your way to find Jesus this morning?"

"Sure, Mom. It won't take long."

"I'd love to stay and help," Steven's father said, finishing his morning juice. "I just love to salt fish—the feel, the texture, the aroma!" Steven and his mother laughed as they chased his father with a fish in each hand. "I love you!" his father shouted as they chased him to the door and into the street with the lamb right behind them.

CHAPTER TEN

I t was midmorning when Steven left his house with the lamb. "It's getting warm," Steven said to the lamb. "We'll try to find Valmus and Margaret at the synagogue." Steven felt as if something was different. "Maybe it's a change in the weather." Steven laughed. "The fall storms will be coming soon."

Steven knew it was more than a change in the weather though. It was the city. It was buzzing with excitement. People seemed happy, almost like it was a holiday. As Steven neared the synagogue, he could overhear people talking about Jesus, telling stories of miraculous things they had either heard about or seen Jesus do. The name of Jesus was on everyone's tongue. As Steven was nearing the synagogue, the excitement grew. Steven and the lamb had become entranced by hearing all the people talk about Jesus. They were listening more to where they were going rather than watching.

Suddenly, someone grabbed his arm in the crowded street. "Hey, partner." Steven knew the voice in an instant. "I was just going home to find you," his father said.

"Hey, Dad. I was just on my way to the synagogue to find you. And Valmus. And Margaret, of course."

"I saw them," Steven's father said. "They're both at the synagogue. But I was going home to tell you we've got to leave for Jerusalem immediately."

"Today!" Steven cried. "I can't go today. He's here. Or someplace close to here. Valmus heard Jesus was close to Capernaum, and I've got to find him."

"I know, Steven," his father patiently replied. "But the religious leaders, the city, everyone, I guess, is in such a frenzy about Jesus. The leaders are sending messages every day. Sometimes more than one, and there are just so many messengers. They're not even sending parchments. I wish they could get as excited about the poor and the hungry and their job as they are about Jesus, who's trying to help and apparently doing a better job than they are!" His father's eyes were fixed on Steven and the lamb, but he didn't see them, and the rise in his voice gave way to the frustration he was feeling. Steven and the lamb stood staring in wide-eyed amazement at the display that was so out of character for his father.

"Okay, Dad," Steven said, still surprised. "Yeah, sure. We'll be ready right away."

Steven's father immediately focused back on them. "Listen, you two," his father said as he knelt down eye level with Steven. "I'm sorry. All of this exposure Jesus is getting concerns me. I believe he can help us. There wouldn't be so many wonderful reports of things he's done if he couldn't. But I'm not sure how the religious leaders are going to react and what the consequences could be. And that worries me." Time stood still. Again, Steven's father was a million miles away.

"Nonetheless," his father finally said with his familiar smile and tone, "we're heading to Jerusalem. And don't worry, Steven. There are reasons for everything. Anyway, I'm sure we'll be back in a matter of days."

Steven's father stood. "Go ahead and take those parcels to Valmus, Margaret, and the others. I'll meet you at home." He turned to continue his way home and was lost in the crowd.

Steven and the lamb exchanged puzzled looks and began making their way to the synagogue. Steven moved slower this time, reflecting on what had just happened with his father. He didn't understand the concern, much less the consequences.

"If I didn't know you'd been here before, I'd say you were lost." It wasn't until he heard his friend's voice that Steven recalled where he was and what he was doing.

"Valmus, it just doesn't make any sense."

"No." Valmus chuckled. "But you'll get used to it."

"Why would there be consequences for doing good things? Doesn't everyone want good things to happen?"

"You would think so, Steven. Why are you asking? Are you in trouble?"

"No. Dad said the religious leaders were getting all concerned about the things Jesus is doing, how he's helping people. You know, giving them hope, something to look forward to."

"Ah, yes," Valmus replied. "All the things the religious leaders can't do. Sometimes people focus more on breaking the rules and consequences than keeping the rules and praise and rewards. That's not the worst problem. I've heard things here at the synagogue. No matter how good the things are Jesus is doing, no matter how much he is able to help people, no matter if he is the Messiah, the chosen one we've been waiting hundreds of years for, he's taking the attention away from the leaders. And attention is something the leaders want as much as or more than they want their salaries."

"So, they're jealous?" Steven asked.

"I'm afraid it may be bigger than that, Steven. I'm afraid they may be scared. The leaders may see it as a matter of survival."

"Survival?" Steven exclaimed, more perplexed than ever.

"I've never seen or heard of people so worked up and excited about anything like they are about Jesus. I'm afraid he's stealing some very prestigious people's thunder. Just last night I was at the south gate, and a huge group of people, must have been a thousand or more, left for Jerusalem to find Jesus," Valmus said.

"Jerusalem!" Steven replied, almost shouting, making Valmus and the lamb jump. All the puzzling thoughts that clouded his young mind vanished. "I thought you heard Jesus was here, in the east, near Bethsaida." Steven was revived with his familiar vigor and excitement. "We're going to Jerusalem. Today. Right now!"

Almost like a reflex, Steven handed Valmus a small parcel of food and headed down the steps of the synagogue. "I'll see you in a few days, Valmus!" he shouted, bounding two, sometime three steps at a time with the lamb right behind him.

"Take care, my young friends!" Valmus yelled back, his good arm stretched out far and high.

Steven and the lamb moved through the crowd of people as if time stood still. They passed by Margaret's water bench, laying another parcel of food down without even stopping. Margaret raised her head, but not in time to see Steven and the lamb. She heard him shout, "Bye, Margaret! See you in a couple days!" Margaret saw the parcel of food and lowered her head back with a smile.

"Bye, Steven. See you in a couple of days," she said softly.

Steven and the lamb made it back to their house in record time. Steven's father was loading a cart in front of their house as Steven and the lamb ran up. "He's going to Jerusalem! I thought he was here! But he's not! I thought I could find him today near the east shore! But Valmus was at the south gate! And a huge group of people left!" Steven's father was beginning to laugh uncontrollably.

"Well, we're ready," his father replied.

Steven's mother appeared from the house. "What could all this excitement possibly be?" she chided with a knowing smile.

"He's going to Jerusalem! And we are too!"

Isa gave the yoke and hitch one more look and a shake, then waited by the side of the cart to help Martha up. Steven had both hands on the wheel and was pulling himself into the back of the cart as the lamb pushed him up and over with his head. His father smiled as he picked up the lamb and held him in his arms. "You two sure make a good pair," he said, scratching the lamb's ears and setting him in the back of the cart. Steven's father climbed onto the cart and took the reins. "Hee up!" he yelled, and the cart slowly began lumbering down the street. Steven was standing behind his father, one arm around his neck and leaning on his back.

"Faster! We've got to go faster!" Steven shouted.

"Easy, partner," his father replied, reaching behind and placing a hand on Steven's neck, pulling him close. "We're lucky to be able to take a cart so we can all go. The leaders are in such turmoil they've just been sending riders."

"That's what I need. A fast horse," Steven said in a most adventurous voice. "I'd run all the way to Jerusalem."

Steven's mother and father laughed as Steven pointed forward. The south gate was in view with the road to Jerusalem behind it. The sun was warm, and the cart made a soft, squeaky noise as they began their journey.

CHAPTER ELEVEN

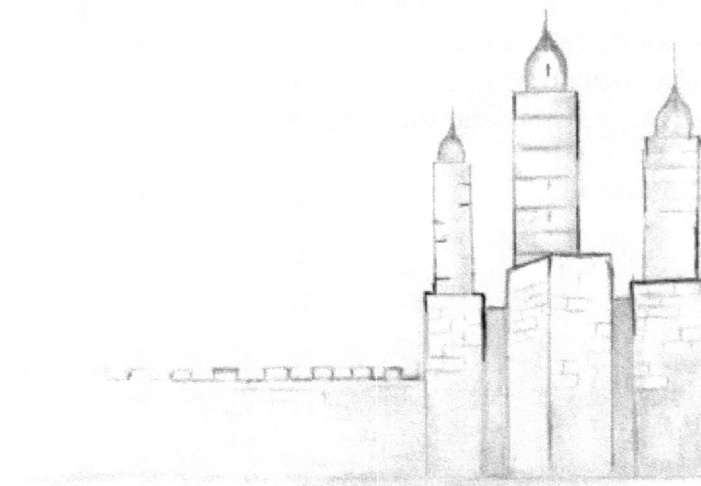

It was absolutely the longest trip to Jerusalem Steven had ever been on, and he had been on quite a few. The lamb lay curled on the bags Steven's family had brought with them, but Steven couldn't sleep.

"How much longer?" he asked with the sound of anxiety and tiredness in his voice.

"Not much farther," his father replied with encouragement. "But you know this road as well as I do. How long will it take to reach the towers from here?"

"About six hours," Steven said. Steven was looking for each marker that helped him determine the time it would take for them to cover the remaining distance. "We just left Sychar, so it should be about six hours." Steven was almost talking to himself.

"Steven, you haven't slept much the entire trip," his mother said. "Why don't you curl up for just a little while? It makes the time go by so much faster. Besides, when you do find Jesus and talk to him, you want to be your best. You don't want to be blurry eyed like you stayed awake from Capernaum to Jerusalem."

Steven yawned. "Maybe just a short nap," he said.

"Your mother's right, Steven," his father added. "And if we hear or see anything, we'll wake you up."

Steven was nestling into the soft bags in the back of the cart as his parents spoke. His head was next to the lamb, which stirred and plopped his head right on top of Steven's. The afternoon sun was warm but not oppressive, and the cart made a rocking motion that sent Steven to the deepest limits of sleep. All was good.

"Steven. Steven, wake up. We're here." Steven roused to his mother's voice and the warm nose nudging his cheek. "Come on, sleepyhead," Steven heard his mother say as the nudging became more persistent, followed by a tug on his ear.

"Okay, okay!" Steven cried as he sat up and rolled the lamb in his lap just like a puppy. "You're a bossy rascal, aren't you?" Steven said, laughing as he continued to roll the lamb in the soft bags he had been lying on.

"He doesn't want you to miss a thing, does he?" Steven's father said as he unfastened the latches that allowed the back gate of the wagon to drop.

"These two are quite a pair, aren't they?" May said as she hugged her sister. Steven moved onto the gate of the wagon letting his legs dangle and then jumped to the ground. The lamb was right behind him. "Of course, I'm sure you've heard that before," she said, taking Steven's cheeks in her hands and kissing him on the top of his head.

Steven looked down the street as his aunt greeted the lamb, then she and his father began unloading the wagon and carrying bags into the house. There were still a few torches burning in front of doors, but the street was silent. Steven was not exactly sure how he felt as he gained his bearings. It was a mix of uncertainty, expectancy, and fear.

"Steven, hop back up there and hand those bags in the front back here," he heard his father say, returning to the wagon from the open door of the house.

"Where is everybody?" Steven asked as his father helped him back up on the gate of the wagon. "Everyone's door is closed. There's no one in the street. No music. It's not that late, is it?" Steven sleepily grabbed the two remaining bags in the front of the wagon and slid them back to his father.

"It's the unknown, Steven. People are scared of the unknown. That's why people are scared of the dark."

"I'm not scared of the dark," Steven arrogantly replied to his father as he boldly stood on the rear of the wagon.

"It's not the dark that people are afraid of, Steven," his father replied. He smiled as he looked up at Steven, who had struck the pose of a seaman on the bow of his vessel facing a violent sea. "It's what's *in* the dark that people are afraid of. What they can't see and can't understand."

"I'm not scared of anything," Steven continued as he increased the boldness of his stance.

"And that's part of what makes you a very special boy," Steven's father said, laughing as he grabbed Steven's legs, bending him over his shoulder and spinning him around before setting him on the ground next to the lamb that was waiting patiently. "But it's what's on the inside that can scare you most," Steven's father continued, leaning toward him with both hands on his shoulders, smiling widely. "Take this lamb, for example. There's a certain element of fear involved with him, is there not?"

Steven's expression had changed to deep concern before his father had finished the sentence. "Yes. I can't lose him.

I just can't," Steven replied. "I've got to talk to Jesus and soon."

"Well, you might be in luck," his father replied in a happier tone, squeezing Steven's shoulder in one hand and leaning to take the lamb's head in the other. Steven's father stood and nonchalantly grabbed the remaining two bags from the back of the wagon and turned toward the door. "Your aunt May said Jesus was in Jerusalem today."

"He's here?" Steven's voice echoed down the street as he turned and caught his father at the entrance of the house.

"Steven!" he heard his mother call from inside the dwelling. "You'll wake the whole side of the city."

"He's here?" Steven continued in a quieter voice. "Why didn't you say something? I've got to find him." The lamb raced into the house in the excitement as Steven began to recognize the uneasy feeling in his stomach he was so familiar with when he faced the idea of talking to Jesus.

Steven's father laughed as he walked past him into the house. "I did. We just got here." He heard his father chuckle as he took the bags to the ladies in the kitchen.

Steven remained at the door with his back to the entrance. "Steven, what's the matter?" his mother asked. Steven, consumed with thoughts of what might happen, did not respond.

"Hey, sport," he heard his father say in his familiar, warm voice. Steven felt his father's large hands knead into both shoulders. "Remember," his father continued, "the people who usually get what they want in life are the people who show up to get it." Steven's father rubbed his shoulders lovingly, yet deep and hard. "I'm sure you'll show up at just the right place, at just the right time."

Steven's mother and aunt had walked to the door, and he felt their touch on his shoulders also.

"Steven, great things are happening. Miracles. Things that have never happened before and that no one can explain," he heard his aunt say. "Never lose faith in that."

"That's right, Steven," his mother said. "Keep your faith."

Steven's father broke the embrace and walked toward the cart. "Well, we've got two tired animals here that need some water and rest," Steven's father said. "Why don't you and your lamb go with me to the stable? I don't think you'll be sleeping any time soon," he said as he pulled himself up onto the wagon. Steven's expression did not change as he walked to the wagon. He helped the lamb aboard and then followed.

"We'll be back shortly, love!" Isa called.

Standing in the doorway, Steven's mother silently raised her hand. Steven's father shook a wave down the reigns, and the cart jerked to a start. Steven sat quietly, holding the lamb, with his father's arm around his shoulders. The only sounds to be heard were hooves on the stone path and the creak of the wagon as they moved down the street lit by only a few remaining torches.

CHAPTER TWELVE

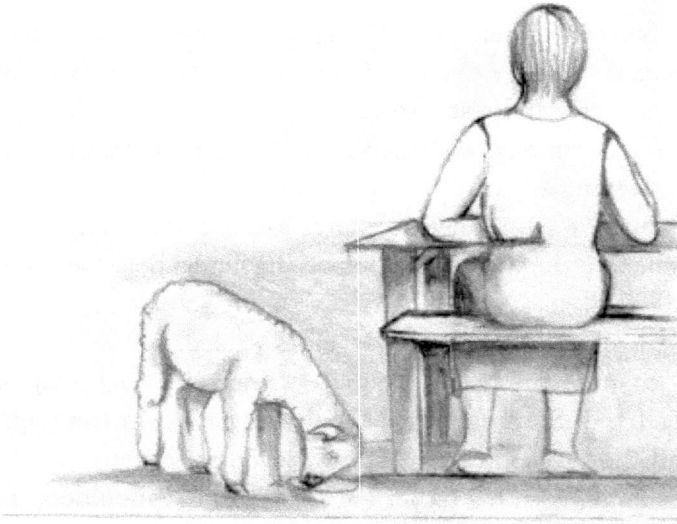

Steven woke from an uneasy sleep. The lamb was still curled on the bed, but voices could be heard from the front part on the house. Steven sat on the edge of the bed, putting his feet on the floor.

"Come on, sleepy," he said to the lamb. "We've got a lot to do. Today may be the day." Steven ran his fingers through the soft fleece on the lamb's back, causing a rippling effect in its muscles and skin. The lamb responded by slowly raising its head and yawning extremely wide with its tongue sticking out and its ears pointing back.

"Mercy, you're a sight in the morning. Can you stay little for the rest of your life? What am I going to do with you when you have horns bigger than you are?" Steven asked, watching the lamb finish a stretch, which resembled a cat. Suddenly the lamb ran, hit Steven with all four hooves, and ricocheted to the floor.

"Why you!" Steven laughed as the lamb ran back in front of him, batting his eyelashes and then making three hops sideways. "I'm excited too. Let's go find Maundi. We've got a lot to tell him, and he may know where we can find Jesus."

"Good morning, Steven." "Hello, you two," came the greetings from his mother and aunt as he entered the kitchen.

"Did you sleep well?" his aunt continued.

"You mean, did you sleep at all?" his mother chided, smiling and hugging him close. "Have you made a plan? Are you ready for the day? Surely today will be the day you have a chance to talk to Jesus."

"I'm ready," Steven replied. "I think you're right. Today is the day. But if Jesus was here yesterday, what if he goes somewhere else today? He's been moving and preaching throughout the region so much lately. I might not ever find him."

"Steven, that doesn't sound like you. What happened to 'anything's possible,' or, 'I can do anything'?"

"I know, Mom. But I'm so worried Jesus will say I need to give the lamb back, that I can't keep him."

"I know, Steven," his mother said, hugging him close again. "The same God who said not to kill said not to worry, Steven. I know it's easier said than done, but that's the challenge."

"But what if he says no?" Steven said into his mother's embrace.

"That's what you've got to find out," his mother replied, taking him by both shoulders. "And you're just the man for the job. Why don't you get a bite to eat while May and I finish the parcels for our friends? You can make your search while you deliver them."

"I will," Steven said more enthusiastically. "I've got so much to tell Maundi, and he probably knows just where Jesus is or where he's going to be."

"Good," his mother said. "There's food on the table, and here's a bowl of grain for your partner."

Steven ate quietly while the two women chatted and laughed with each other as they packed the parcels Steven was to deliver. He ate figs, olives, bread, and a piece of smoked fish without even paying attention to the food. The lamb stood beside him, crunching the grain Steven had put in front of him.

Steven's thoughts were consumed with having the full attention of Jesus and telling how he came into the possession of the lamb. He rehearsed and edited his conversation over and over.

"What was that, Steven? Steven?"

"Yes, Mom."

"You said something."

"Oh, it's nothing. I was just thinking out loud."

The women laughed. "That's why it's a good idea to always watch what you're thinking." His aunt chuckled.

"I know what you were thinking, and you'll be fine, Steven," his mother said.

"Thanks, Mom. I hope you're right. Where's Dad?"

"He's already gone to the temple. He was to be there first thing." Steven grabbed the wrap containing the food parcels his mother and aunt had prepared. "I guess it was a pretty important scroll someone needed for a lesson, huh?"

"No scroll this time, Steven. Just messages. The leaders seem to be in such a twit. I've never seen them act so upset."

"Valmus says they're jealous of Jesus," said Steven. "And they don't understand, so that makes them scared." Steven's mother smiled and hugged him close once more before he left.

"You're probably right, Steven. You're probably right. And, Steven?" his mother said, kneeling in front of him. "If Jesus doesn't come to Jerusalem today, there will be a time. Don't go outside the walls by yourself."

"I know, Mom. The dogs. I won't forget about the dogs." Steven headed to the door with the parcels of food and the lamb at his side. "Maundi says there are dogs in the city, too. Just a different kind," he said with his back to the women.

"That may be true!" his mother called. "But they won't tear you to shreds." Steven's mother followed him to the door. "Promise me, Steven!" his mother called again.

"I promise," Steven said, waving back to his mother as he continued walking.

"Tell everyone hello for us."

"I will," he replied, not missing a step.

"I love you!" she called one last time.

"Love you too, Mom!" Steven yelled back as he and the lamb disappeared into the morning.

"He's so reckless," his mother said to her sister as she closed the door.

"Remember what a daredevil Isa was when he was that age?" May laughed. "I think that's why you liked him so much." Both women laughed as they began clearing the food from the table.

CHAPTER THIRTEEN

S teven made his way through the Essene Quarter with
a more determined sense of urgency. He took his most
familiar trail to see his friend Maundi first—past the the-
atre, up the stairs at Robinson's Arch, around the Royal
Porch, and through the sheep gate to the pool of Bethesda.
The city was more crowded than usual because of the
celebration.

Steven looked along the way for signs of gatherings
indicating Jesus's presence but saw none. He made the
entire trip talking to no one. Soon after passing the Israel
pool, the five covered colonnades surrounding the pool of
Bethesda came into view. Steven quickened his pace with
the anticipation of seeing Maundi.

People of all shapes, sizes, and expectancy usually surrounded the pool, patiently waiting for the water to stir.
But today there was barely a few. Steven walked toward the
side of the pool where Maundi waited and immediately
noticed he was nowhere to be seen. Steven ran at first and
then slowly walked to the place where Maundi had always
rested on his mat.

Steven scanned the area around the pool and then
turned and looked behind him. "Maundi!" Steven shouted.
"Maundi!" he shouted again, turning to face the pool.

"He's not here!" he heard an old, feeble voice screech at
him from across the pool. Steven saw the old woman with

the extremely hunched back on the other side of the pool. "I didn't come one day, just one day, and he came," she continued. "Now everyone's well—or almost everyone."

"Who came?" Steven shouted back.

"They said he didn't say his name. They said he brought gifts from God. They said he called God 'Father,' and I wasn't here. I didn't come, and I wasn't here."

Steven began to slowly approach the woman as she spoke. He was close enough to see tears running down her face when he stopped.

"It was the Sabbath, and I wasn't here," she said, hanging her head.

"It was Jesus," Steven said in a quiet voice. "Jesus is the only one who could do this. He can help you, too," he assured the woman. "I'm going to find him. I'll tell him. I'll tell him you're here."

The old woman put her hand on Steven's shoulder. "Please, son. Please find him." Steven handed the woman a parcel of food, which she took with her other hand. "Bless you, son," she said. "Bless you, and Godspeed." Steven silently turned and hurried back the way he had come with the lamb right at his side.

Steven's heart raced just as fast as he and the lamb traveled back toward the temple. His mind was a blur as thoughts came from everywhere about what might have taken place. He was completely oblivious to the sounds and smells of the city as he made his fastest time ever back toward the temple.

Steven and the lamb had just turned back on a main street when a huge splash of water landed right in front of them. Steven slowed, but before he could look up to see where the water had come from, he and the lamb were showered with torrents of water. Steven was knocked to one knee and rested on his hand in the mud. He looked for the lamb that had just started a shake, which started in his nose and ended in his tail. Before he stood, Steven heard the laughter and knew what had happened.

"Well, we knew if we waited long enough we'd catch some poor fool unawares." The boys on the wall roared with laughter, looking down at Steven and the lamb standing in the muddy spot in the street. "We sure didn't think we'd be lucky enough to catch you not looking!" Judi shouted over the other boys' laughter.

Judi wasn't laughing. He wasn't even coming close to smiling as he looked down from the wall. "Why don't you wait right there? We should probably get that lamb back where he belongs."

"This is my lamb!" Steven shouted, looking up at Judi and stepping forward. "Jesus gave him to me!" A wave of emotion came over Steven that was almost uncontrollable. He felt his hands roll into fists and a power surge through his arms.

"Steven, you're such a schmuck. Jesus gave you that lamb? Just because a guy can make a mess in my father's temple and do a lot of fancy tricks doesn't mean he has any right to give you that lamb."

The other boys had quieted their laughter as Judi continued. "All these tricks and games are coming to an end soon anyway. My father almost had the Roman soldiers break your crippled friend's new legs if he didn't tell him who fixed them. Ends up it was this Jesus doing more tricks and telling people it's okay to break the laws. Now that will never do." Judi's face had twisted into a sneer that was the closest Steven had ever seen to a smile.

Steven was suddenly aware that he was soaking wet. He felt cold, and a lump rose in his throat, which made it hard to breathe, much less swallow. Steven wanted to shout at Judi, but he couldn't. He wanted to tell Judi he was wrong and that he didn't have any idea what he was saying, but he couldn't speak. As the boys on the wall filed down the narrow stairway that led to the street below, the lamb nudged Steven's leg. Although he wanted to stay and fight, Steven knew what the results would be and what would be at risk for the lamb.

Looking down at the lamb, Steven turned and ran. He ran faster than before, faster than he had ever run. He ran past the golden gate along the west side of the temple. He ran to the Royal Porch and through the Huldah Gate toward the upper city. Steven thought of nothing. His concerns of Maundi, of Jesus, of what had happened before at the pool, and what had just happened with Judi and his friends completely disappeared. The only thing in Steven's mind was to run. As Steven approached his aunt's house, he ran into the open arms of his father, who was just leaving for the temple.

"Whoa again there, partner!" Steven felt the arms that had held him, loved him, and protected him his whole life. Steven's father could tell right away something was wrong by the way Steven clung to him and pressed his face into his chest. "Steven, what's wrong? What is it? Are Judi and those other boys picking on you again?"

Steven didn't answer. "Steven, I'm on my way to the temple right now. I think it's time we said something to Judi's father. He can't do this every time we come to Jerusalem, even if he is the high priest's—," Steven quietly cut his father short, still holding on tightly.

"It's the lamb. He wants the lamb. He said he was going to kill him."

Steven's father was silent. Steven stepped back from his father. His face was wet, not with tears, but sweat, and he was still breathing hard.

His father recognized the look in his eyes and then heard it in his voice. "We've got to go. Now."

There was a pause as the two exchanged feelings and understanding; then Steven's father spoke. "We will. We'll leave right away. May and your mother are getting things ready right now. I've got to go to the temple, and then we'll leave right away."

"Don't say anything. Please. Don't say anything about Judi or what happened or the lamb or anything. I've got to find Jesus." Steven's father pulled him close once again. "I've got to ask him. He'll tell them he's mine. He'll tell them I can keep him."

"Don't worry, Steven," his father replied. "We'll work it out. It will all be okay." With that, Steven went into the house, and his father left for the temple.

Chapter Fourteen

The trip back to Capernaum was a quiet one. Neither Steven nor his parents made much conversation, only comments about people or things they saw along the way. Steven knew his parents spoke softly when they thought he was sleeping. He heard them mention Jesus and recognized the concern in their voices.

The farther they traveled from Jerusalem, the farther Steven's mind drifted from the episode with Judi and the viciousness in which he had acted. His thoughts bounced almost with the cart from Maundi, to the woman at the pool, to Caiaphas. *Is Maundi okay? Does the high priest want the lamb back?*

It wasn't until they neared Capernaum that Steven engaged his parents. "Maundi wasn't at the pool," Steven said, breaking the silence except for the hooves of the oxen and sound of the carts wheels on the road.

"No," his father finally replied. "No, I understand he wasn't. I heard Jesus was in Jerusalem for the feast and more wonderful things happened."

Steven shifted his weight on the bags in the back of the wagon as the lamb, tired of riding and ready to play, jumped off the bags with all four feet onto Steven's back and then down to the floor of the cart. Steven reached and petted the lamb but did not continue the play the lamb had initiated.

"And some of these wonderful things occurred on the Sabbath. Is that correct?" Steven's parents looked at each other, and his mother turned to him in a more comfortable position.

"That's what we heard," she said in a calm, collected voice.

"Are the religious leaders mad?" Steven asked sullenly. "Judi said Maundi could walk. A woman at the pool said it happened on the Sabbath, and then Judi said his dad was going to hurt Maundi if he didn't tell him in front of all the religious leaders at the temple who healed him."

Steven's father turned, holding the reigns in his left hand. "There was some sort of altercation at the temple involving Maundi. And he can walk!" he exclaimed.

"Were you there?" Steven quickly asked. "Did you see him?"

"No. And no," his father replied. "But I was told that Maundi is in the south part of the city and that he's safe. He's okay. No, he's more than okay. He's wonderful!" his father continued with more enthusiasm than had been expressed on their whole journey. "For most of his life, Maundi has been sitting by that pool, unable to even help himself when the waters stirred. Now they say he has the legs of a young man!" Steven's father was almost shouting to the countryside as they neared the city.

The lamb joined in the excitement and jumped in Martha's lap. Steven's expression didn't change. Steven's mother and father played with the lamb, relieved the mood had changed and that they were nearing home. Steven sat quietly, recognizing familiar signs as they were getting closer to their destination.

"The religious leaders *are* angry," Steven said, breaking a pause in the action. A shadow of gloom seemed to cover them again as the cart creaked along. "That's why you're making so many trips back and forth to Jerusalem, isn't it? The religious leaders are mad, and they don't know what to do, do they?"

They sat quietly without looking at one another, and Steven's father finally spoke. "There does seem to be some anxiety among some of the leaders. Some say he's blaspheming when he says he's the Son of God, but the prophets spoke of this. Some say he's only after attention, but no one can explain the miraculous things he does, and the prophets spoke of this. Everything seems to be happening just as it was written, but some have trouble recognizing just what's happening. It's almost as if there's a conflict of interest. It's almost as if the leaders feel Jesus's message threatens the law, leaving the leaders powerless."

"But Jesus has said he's not here to threaten the law, the leaders, or anyone," Steven's mother said with an aggravated voice.

They rode quietly, and Steven's father spoke again. "We've heard it read from Isaiah many times, 'He was despised and rejected by men, a man of sorrows, and familiar with suffering.'" The three looked at each other.[7]

"'He was pierced for our transgressions. He was crushed for our iniquities,'" Martha said, looking at Isa.[8]

"Remember what John said?" Steven added sadly. His mother and father turned to him as he spoke. "'Look, the

Lamb of God who takes away the sin of the world.' And we all know what they do with lambs," he said, looking down. The ride into the city was silent, but it was good to be home.[9]

Evening was just beginning to fall as they reached their house. Steven and the lamb jumped from the cart and headed down the street toward the synagogue.

"Steven, where are you going?" his mother asked.

"I've got to find him. Maybe he's here in the city," Steven said, turning and walking backward as he spoke.

"Steven," his mother and father said simultaneously.

"Steven, don't leave this city," his mother continued.

"Okay!" Steven called as he turned and hurried down the street.

"Be back at dark," his father added.

"Okay, Dad!" Steven called back.

"Don't leave this city!" Steven heard his mother shout as he disappeared into the maze of people and buildings.

CHAPTER FIFTEEN

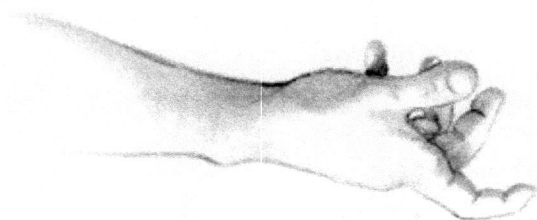

B ut he's out there somewhere. Out by the Sea of Galilee," Steven argued with his mother.

"I know," his mother calmly replied.

"Crowds leave every day to go to him. Sera and I used
to go almost that far by ourselves when she was feeling
good," he continued in a pleading voice.

Steven's mother shot a glare at him. "Well, I was certainly unaware of that, young man."

"I could stay with the crowds. It's been days, and Jesus
hasn't been in Capernaum once."

"I know, Steven," she replied calmly again, continuing
with her work.

"People have told Valmus that he's there. Uncle Simon
and Uncle Andrew are there. I could stay with them," Steven continued, sounding more agitated.

Steven's mother stopped and turned to him with a look
of frustration and concern. "Steven," she said slowly as if
choosing her words wisely, "there is no one to go with you
right now. Your father will be back soon. I don't want you
to go alone."

"But, Mom!" Steven interjected.

"I don't want you to go alone or in a crowd," she said in
a sterner voice.

"I'm tired of waiting," Steven said, exasperated, turning
toward the door.

Martha reached him at the door, hugging him close, pulling his back to her chest. "Remember it's God's story, Steven, not yours. Things happen how and when God wants them to. Promise me," she said.

"I promise," Steven finally replied.

"Now have a good day," she said cheerfully, swatting him on the rump and handing him a wrap of food parcels to be delivered. "You never know. Today might just be the day." Steven smiled a crooked smile at his mother as she bent and rubbed the lamb's cheeks and then scratched its ears. "Keep him out of harm's way," she said to the lamb as Steven and the lamb headed out the door. "Be careful!" she called. "I love you!"

"Love you too, Mom!" Steven yelled back.

It was truly a beautiful morning, as had been the mornings of the last several weeks. Steven was tired of waiting, but today was the day after the Sabbath, and Jesus could very well be in Capernaum. Steven's excitement continued to grow as he and the lamb neared the main entrance of the city to see Valmus.

He had a lot planned for today. He would make his usual stops to see Valmus and Margaret and had plans to see Sera if he could. He had been so busy the past few weeks he had not gone by to see her. The news was that she had still not improved; so, he was going to check in with Rosetta today for sure.

Steven was so lost in thought that he was standing at the main entrance before he realized it. Something was definitely different though. He turned to the place Valmus had stood every morning for years. He turned in a full circle looking, but Valmus wasn't there. Steven stepped through the gate and looked, but no sign of Valmus. He turned and ran. "He must be at the synagogue already," he said to the lamb as they worked their way through the crowds of people beginning to gather.

As Steven and the lamb approached the steps of the synagogue, it was obvious something was happening. It was like a festival. People were rejoicing and singing, and great joy was being expressed everywhere.

"Margaret! What's going on?" Steven exclaimed upon reaching the woman sitting on bags under her colorful tent.

By now, Steven's stomach was completely tied in knots. The idea that Jesus might be at the synagogue or nearby gave Steven the all-too-familiar anxious feelings. He could barely speak.

"Oh, Steven. It's wonderful. He was here. Jesus was here yesterday afternoon. It was just after you and your mother left for home. He was here and did such wonderful things."

"Is Valmus here?" asked Steven.

"Yes, he's here. He's waiting inside for you. He said you would be here early today. It's wonderful, Steven. Valmus's hand is whole. It's brand new. Oh, Steven, I wish you could have been here. I know you want to talk to him, and he was right here."

"What about you, Margaret? Did you approach Jesus and ask for help?"

"No, Steven. I could never do that. I was shaking so hard just being near him I could hardly move. I could never approach him for help."

"But he loves you, Margaret. Jesus loves everyone. He wants you to be well."

"I'm sure he does, Steven, but I could never ask for help. Besides, sometimes the crowds get so worked up that I could never get close enough to ask. I don't understand how Jesus can move through crowds like that and not have them pressing against him."

"That's it, Margaret. Reach through the crowd and touch Jesus. I believe that would work. Reach through and touch him, knowing he loves you and wants you to be well."

"Oh, Steven. You're probably right. I know he can help me. I'm just not worthy to ask." Steven set a parcel of food down on the bench by Margaret's water jar. He then leaned over and gave the woman a big hug.

"I know the feeling, Margaret. I know the feeling."

Margaret hugged Steven back and kissed him on the cheek. "Bless you, Steven. Now go find Valmus. He's waiting for you." Steven and the lamb turned and began their ascent up the steps to the synagogue.

They reached the top in record time. Valmus again was not in his usual place. When he was not at one of the gates, Valmus was usually found at the top the steps right out in the open, almost as if greeting everyone that came into the synagogue. Steven saw small groups of people hugging and rejoicing together. He saw religious leaders scurrying around.

Toward the inner part of the synagogue, Steven could see a larger group of people. He thought at first someone might be reading, but the more he looked, people were coming and going. Steven and the lamb walked in the direction of the attraction and heard people talking as they got closer.

"I've known him his whole life," he heard a woman say.

"His arm has never been right. Now look at it!" Steven heard another say.

Working his way through the crowd, he reached the focus of all the attention and excitement. There sat Valmus. People circled around him, looking and then moving on so others could pass by. Steven approached and was beside him before Valmus realized it.

"Valmus?"

"Steven!" Valmus roared. "I've been waiting! How are you? Look. Look what Jesus did for me. Did you talk to Jesus yesterday?" Valmus stood as he was talking and wrapped both arms around Steven, picked him up, and spun him around. "I've been wanting to do this your whole life," Valmus said.

"No," Steven replied, laughing, "I didn't see him. I didn't even know he was here." He continued laughing and speaking in a constricted voice from Valmus's hug.

"I thought you talked to him and asked him to come help me," Valmus said, setting Steven back to the ground and picking up the lamb and cradling him in his arms. "Jesus got to the synagogue shortly after you and your mother left yesterday. He came in, and the leaders were on him immediately. They started asking if it was *law-*

ful"—Valmus stressed and drew out the word—"to do the wonderful things he does on the Sabbath. Can you believe that?" he exclaimed. "But he told them." Valmus continued, "He asked them, 'If any of you had a sheep,'" Valmus said, holding the lamb up a bit, which nuzzled him on the chin. "'If any of you had a sheep and it fell into a pit'"—Valmus suddenly dropped his arms enough to make the lamb's eyes fly open with surprise— "'would you not take hold of it and lift it out?'" Valmus stood and cradled the lamb in his arms again. "'How much more valuable is a man than a sheep,'" he continued. "'Therefore it is lawful to do good on the Sabbath.' Then he turned right to me and said, 'Stretch out your hand.' And when I did, it was whole! Brand new! Perfect!" Valmus set the lamb down and showed Steven his arm, opening and closing his hand as he spoke.[10] The large group of people who had crowded around them pressed closer while Valmus talked to Steven and showed him his arm and hand.

"Steven," Valmus said with a completely different tone of voice, "we were talking about Sera. You must go see her. I heard she is worse. I'm staying here to show people what Jesus has done for me. People have to see what Jesus can do, so they, too, will believe."

"Okay, Valmus. We'll leave right now. I'm sure we'll see you soon." Steven turned to leave and then looked back at Valmus. "Jesus could help Sera," he said.

"Indeed he could," Valmus replied with a smile. "Indeed he could."

Steven and the lamb worked their way through the crowd to the steps at the front of the synagogue. As they were leaving, Steven noticed a group of religious leaders huddled together. They seemed to be having a heated discussion and were not very happy.

It was a perfect day. The walk to Sera's house reminded Steven of when they used to play together. He used to walk this path frequently, but it had been a while.

Steven hurried up the brick streets to Sera's house and was soon knocking on the huge wooden door at the entrance. Rosetta arrived shortly but did not greet them with a smile. She bent and hugged Steven. "Oh, Steven, it's good to see you."

The look on Rosetta's face told Steven immediately, but he finally asked, "How's Sera?"

"Not good, Steven. Not good. She's still not improving, and it seems she's gotten weaker."

"I'm sorry, Rosetta," Steven said, looking down.

"I know she would love to see you," Rosetta said as she struggled with a smile. "But I'm afraid she's just too weak." The smile disappeared and the concerned look quickly returned.

"I understand," said Steven. "You know?" he continued. "I haven't had an opportunity to talk to Jesus yet. But I know he could help Sera. I know he could. I will find him. I'll ask him. I will."

Rosetta smiled again. "Thank you, Steven," she said. "He may be our only hope."

"I'll find him," Steven said again, turning toward the door. "I heard he's in the country out by the sea, but he was just here, in Capernaum. He healed my friend, Valmus. Jesus made his hand brand new. I know he can help Sera." By this time, Steven and the lamb were outside the large wooden door. "I'll find him," Steven said, turning back to Rosetta.

"Thank you, Steven," Rosetta said, looking down and closing the door behind Steven and the lamb.

Steven turned and ran toward home. He ran with a whole new feeling, though. He had to find Jesus. Before it had been his own desire to keep the lamb, but now there were other lives at stake.

Chapter Sixteen

M om, I have to go!" Steven exclaimed. "It's Sera, and I know Jesus can help her."

"I really believe he can," Steven's mother replied. "I just don't want you to go alone."

"You know I won't be alone, Mom. There are lots of people going out to find Jesus, to listen to him and ask for help."

"But he'll probably be here in the city any day now," she said, looking at Steven and the lamb, knowing she was losing ground.

"He was here just a couple of days ago. Valmus has a brand-new hand, but we didn't see him," Steven argued.

"Yes. Isn't that wonderful?" she replied, busying herself with her work.

"That we didn't see him?" Steven asked.

"No," his mother replied, turning to Steven, knowing he was going to have to go. "That Jesus helped Valmus. And I know Jesus can help Sera, too," she said, kneeling down and looking Steven in the eyes. "But Steven," she said, taking hold of his shoulders, "you mustn't be by yourself. Watch out for the dogs. Always stay with someone. Don't take the trails down to the beach and the shortcuts."

"I'll be careful, Mom," said Steven. "Dad and I've done this hundreds of times. I know just what to do."

"I know, Steven. You're a smart boy," she said, changing her hold on Steven's shoulders to a hug around his neck. "But you've never gone alone, and it worries me, and I want to go with you, but I can't," she said with her face in Steven's shoulder.

"It's okay, Mom. We'll be fine," he said, returning the hug.

"Okay," his mother replied, gaining her composure. "You'll be fine. And you take care of him," she said to the lamb who had rubbed against her. "Take your robe and this food, and hurry right home." Steven gathered his things, and he and the lamb headed for the door.

"We'll be back before you know it," he told his mother.

"Okay. Be safe. Find Simon and Andrew, and stay with them. Stay with a group while you're walking."

"Don't worry, Mom," Steven said, hugging his mother again. "We'll be right back."

Steven and the lamb headed down the street toward the main gate. He waved back to his mother, who was still watching as the two strode away. Steven had walked down this street a thousand times, but he had never felt like he did right now in his whole life. It was almost as if it was the first time. He felt so grown up yet so vulnerable.

There were always people coming and going at the gates. It wouldn't be hard to find someone who was going out to the countryside by the sea. "Come on, boy," Steven said to the lamb, quickening his pace. "We've got some ground to cover."

There weren't as many people leaving the gate as Steven had hoped. A family of five finally came along with a woman who had a hurt leg. Steven decided to leave with them. He looked back at the gate like he had many times before while traveling with his father, but it still felt brand new. "Stay close," he said to the lamb as the city slowly faded from sight.

Steven had mixed feelings as they traveled along. He felt the anticipation of his quest and the excitement of knowing he was walking in the footsteps of Jesus on the very road he traveled. But they were moving so slowly. Steven soon learned the woman had started having trouble with her knees years ago, and it had grown steadily worse.

The group talked constantly of Jesus and what they had seen and heard. "I know he can help me if I can just get close enough to ask," the woman said, stopping to rest her legs again.

"I'm sure he can," Steven replied, telling her about Maundi and how he had not been able to walk at all for so many years.

"Yes! Yes. We've heard so many wonderful things," she said excitedly, walking again with new vigor.

"It's getting so hard to approach him now. So many people are going to him," said the old man in the group.

"We had a friend whose legs would not work at all, much like your friend in Jerusalem," said a young woman. "Jesus was in the city, and we couldn't get our friend close enough to ask for help," she continued as they moved slowly along. "Jesus was in a house that was full. No one else could fit in the house, so we made a hole in the roof and lowered him down to Jesus."[11]

"Right down through the roof?" asked Steven.

"Yes!" replied the woman. "And it worked. Jesus made «him whole. He can walk fine, like a new man. It's wonderful the things Jesus can do for people!" she said with great excitement.

"That's why we're on our way," the old woman replied.

"Why don't you wait until Jesus comes back to Capernaum to ask for help?" Steven asked. "That way it won't hurt so bad to walk all this way."

"Probably the same reason you're here," said the old man. "Jesus can help you and your friend Sera, but there's a certain amount of effort you have to put into it. It's different for every person."

This made Steven think. He thought about just how hard he had tried to find Jesus and all the feelings that had gotten in the way.

Steven looked down the road and saw other groups of people traveling in the same direction far in the distance. The morning was young, so he bid his travel companions goodbye and hurried to catch up with the next group. He and his father had done this many times.

"Be careful and good luck!" called the woman. "Watch out for the wild dogs," was the last thing he heard as he and the lamb ran down the road.

CHAPTER SEVENTEEN

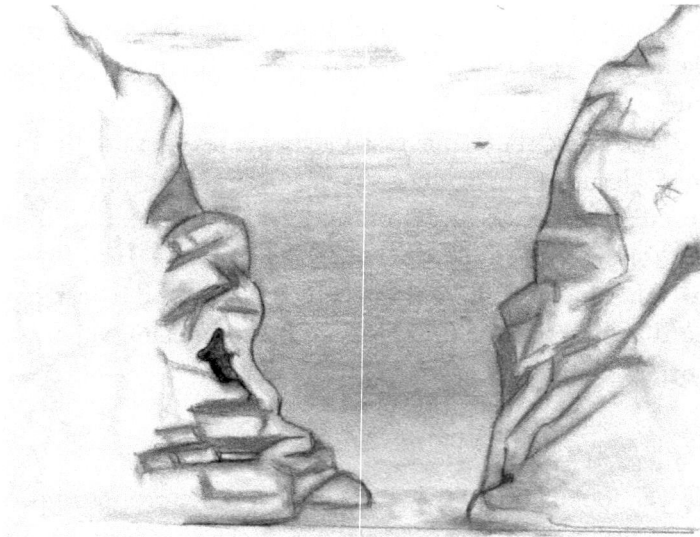

I t didn't take long for Steven to reach the next group of people. This was a larger group who welcomed Steven and the lamb warmly when they finally caught up. They were by the sea at this point. The road wound beside a cliff overlooking the beach and made wide sweeps around deep gashes which had washed out of the cliff wall.

"So you're off to find Jesus too?" asked a man with a limp. He was the first person Steven came up to and was struggling to keep up with the others. "What's your story?"

As they walked along, Steven proceeded to tell the man about Jesus in the temple and getting the lamb, Maundi at the pool, Valmus, and Sera, who so desperately needed Jesus's help. He had just begun to talk about Jesus being the man whom the Scriptures talked about when the man broke his silence and laughed out loud. "But we're expecting a king!" he exclaimed. "We're expecting someone who will rid our land of this Roman influence. Can a man from Galilee do this?" He laughed again.

Steven was silent now. He was fully aware that a king was expected to rescue his people, but he had not looked at Jesus this way. After talking with his friends and family, especially after his first encounter with Jesus in the temple, he looked at Jesus as more of a savior, a man offering hope to those who have none, a man creating opportunities.

Steven was trying to think of a response. There were many thoughts running through his head when he noticed the road was turning away from the cliff again. A trail had been made in the deep ravine down to the beach. Steven knew if he got to the beach, he could make much better time traveling since he would not have to take the road's wide, out-of-the-way sweeps around the deep ravines.

Just as Steven and the man were walking past the trail, Steven looked at the man and with a voice much beyond his years said, "Have you ever known a man from anywhere who can do the things Jesus can?" At this, Steven and the lamb headed down into the ravine toward the beach. The man stopped and watched them disappear but said nothing.

Steven was glad to be on the beach. There were so many interesting things to see and smell, and the small waves made a beautiful sound. "This will save so much time," Steven said as he and the lamb ran close by the water, making footprints in the sand.

The afternoon sun shone brightly as Steven and the lamb walked along. Steven started thinking about what he said to his mother, about leaving the group, and was looking for a trail back up to the main road when he noticed his shadow had disappeared. Ominous clouds had covered the sun and were rolling in fast.

"Looks like it might rain," he said to the lamb. "Let's find that trail and get back with the group."

The wind picked up, and a few raindrops began to fall. Steven and the lamb began running, looking for a trail, when there was a bright flash and a huge crash of thunder. Immediately the wind really started to blow, and the waves that had been making such a pleasant sound earlier were crashing farther and farther up the beach.

Steven and the lamb ran in earnest as rain began to pour from above. They were running closer to the cliff wall, looking for a trail back to the road as waves threatened to cover the entire beach. There seemed to be no escape. Rain blew sideways, and the waves were at their feet. Steven and the lamb desperately hugged the cliff wall, looking for some kind of shelter, when Steven spotted a small cleft in the rocks about five feet up.

The lamb bounded up the small rocks protruding from the wall and waited in the opening as Steven scrambled to get over the edge. The lamb jumped back down into the water and nudged Steven up into the opening and then hopped back up the rocks, following him inside.

Steven and the lamb made their way up and back as far into the opening of the rock as they could. The lamb sat between Steven's legs, and they huddled together, looking out as the sea thrashed and water crashed against the cliff wall. The noise was terrifying, and water began to wash into the hole higher and higher, threatening to wash the two out!

Suddenly, the storm stopped. The wind and rain completely disappeared. Steven and the lamb remained huddled together, filled with fear and unsure of what was happening as sunlight flooded the beach. The only sound they heard was water that had washed ashore trickling back to the sea.

"What is going on?" Steven asked, and he and the lamb began creeping back to the opening of the hole. Steven looked out at the sea, and it was like glass. There was no breeze, and the afternoon sun shone brightly without a cloud in the sky.

"This is amazing," Steven said. He had never seen the sea so calm. Steven and the lamb climbed out of their shelter and walked down to water's edge. There wasn't a single ripple in the water.

Steven stood by the water looking out, and a noise caught his ears. Farther up the beach and out quite a way was a boat, a small vessel, probably a fishing boat. It was too far away to make out who or even how many people there were, but Steven could make out their joyful sounds. He heard them shout and whistle, obviously overjoyed that the storm had disappeared.[12]

A gentle breeze began to blow, which lifted the small boat's sail. The waves of the sea began making their pleasant lapping sound along the beach, and everything seemed just as it had been earlier before the storm.

"Well, lucky for us," Steven said to the lamb. "But I've never seen anything like this before. Let's get back up top and see if anyone knows what happened." Not too much farther down the beach from where they were was another ravine that offered a trail back to the top of the cliff. Soon Steven and the lamb were on the road at the top of the cliff, which was crowded with people walking back toward the city.

"Is Jesus here? Is he with you?" Steven asked a woman in the large group of people.

"No," she replied as he and the lamb walked along. "He was with us before, but he left with his disciples in a boat. I hope they're okay. Wasn't that a freak storm? The worst I've ever seen one minute and the next, completely gone. Just gone," she said with astonishment in her voice.

"So Jesus isn't here in the countryside anymore?" Steven said, not necessarily to anyone.

"No," replied the woman. "We're all heading back to the city," she replied. "You might as well stay along with us. We'll be back before it's completely dark."

Steven walked quietly. It was disappointing that he would not see Jesus today. However, the excitement of traveling out by himself and the amazement of the storm made Steven feel all was not a loss. Besides, if Jesus left in a boat, maybe he was going back to the city, too. Steven had a good feeling in his heart as he and the lamb walked along with the large group of people back toward the city.

Chapter Eighteen

Yes, we were safe. The amazing thing was how fast it stopped."

"Were you with a large group of people?" Steven's mother questioned him.

"At different times the group was pretty big. It was like somebody snapped their fingers, and it was over. Off. Finished."

"Were there plenty of wraps to get under, and did you huddle together?" she asked.

"Well, sort of. Wraps and rocks and lots of shelter. We huddled together. Everyone was fine. It really didn't last that long. And when it stopped, it stopped."

Steven's mother eyed him suspiciously. "God has a way of making his presence known," she said, continuing her wondering look. Steven avoided the look and jumped right in helping his mother with the food parcels she was preparing that morning. "It's funny. It didn't really storm here at all. It's getting close to that time of year, though," she said.

"Is Dad going to be home soon?" Steven asked.

"He should be home today or tomorrow. It depends on if he's got to go to Jericho or someplace else on his return," she replied. "The leaders are sure keeping these guys busy."

"I wish he could stay home for a while," Steven said. "I might find Jesus here in Capernaum, but if Dad was with me, I'm sure we'd find him right away."

Steven's mother laughed. "I'm sure you would."

"I might find him today. He crossed over on a boat yesterday. He might be right here in the city. I've got to check on Sera and see if Jesus will help her."

"Steven!" his mother said quite abruptly. "Do not leave this city."

"I know, Mom. I'm not going anywhere. Besides, by the time I get these delivered and check on Sera, I'll know if Jesus is here or not."

"That's my boy," she said, hugging him close. "Just be careful, and think positive. God helps everybody, but he shines on those who have faith and try to help themselves."

"Okay, Mom," Steven replied as he and the lamb headed out of the door and down the street.

"Stay in the city!" Steven heard his mother call as she waved goodbye.

Steven felt alive this morning. He felt as if anything were possible as he and the lamb bounded down the streets toward the synagogue. He thought this would be the best place to begin his search, as he would probably find Valmus and Margaret there.

Steven was just taking in the sounds of the morning and thinking how this morning seemed peaceful like every other morning when he noticed someone scurrying among the people in the street up ahead. The person wasn't really running, but they were definitely in a hurry. As he got closer, Steven saw that it was Valmus who was in such a rush. He was right upon Steven and the lamb and still hadn't noticed them.

"Valmus?" Steven called to him, but he didn't slow a bit. "Valmus!" Steven called louder. Breathing heavily, Valmus stopped and looked at Steven as if he didn't recognize him.

"Valmus, what's wrong? What is it?" Steven asked urgently.

"Oh, yes. There you are," Valmus replied. "I was just on my way to your house. He's here. Jesus is in Capernaum," Valmus said in between breaths. "It's amazing. Margaret is well! After all these years! She's well!"

"That's great!" Steven said, taking both hands Valmus extended to him. "Tell me everything. What happened?"

"Well," Valmus started, finally catching his breath, "Jairus was at the synagogue early. I thought he was looking after the building and beginning his other duties, but he seemed distant and didn't speak to anyone. Then someone came to the synagogue and said Jesus was on his way to Capernaum by boat. Immediately, a crowd went to meet him at the shore, and when we got there, Jairus worked his way to Jesus and knelt in front of him. He told him Sera was dying, but that he could lay his hands on her and she would live."

"So what happened?" asked Steven.

"Well, Jesus and his disciples left with Jairus," Valmus replied.

"What about Margaret?" Steven asked. "Did she stop Jesus at the shore before he left?"

"No," Valmus replied. "That's what's amazing. A crowd was following Jesus and his disciples, and Margaret reached through and touched Jesus's cloak. She acted, but Jesus turned to her and told her it wasn't her actions. He said, 'Your faith has healed you.' From that moment she was well. It was amazing. Just like what he did for me," "Valmus said excitedly.

"That's wonderful, Valmus. I knew it would work," Steven said. Valmus's joyful expression immediately vanished. "Valmus, what is it?" Steven asked.

"Just as Jesus was talking to Margaret, three men from the house of Jairus arrived and reported that Sera had died and not to bother Jesus."

"Sera died?" Steven exclaimed. "We're too late," he cried angrily.

"I'm not sure, Steven. I do know Jesus went with Jairus." Steven said nothing.

"Steven? Are you okay?" Valmus asked.

Steven replied. "I've got to go. I'll go to Sera's and find out what's happened."

"Yes," Valmus agreed. "You run ahead, and I'll catch up."

"Okay," Steven said, handing Valmus the bag containing the parcels of food he was carrying. "I'll see you there," he said as he and the lamb ran toward Sera's house.

The streets were not crowded at first when Steven and the lamb started off. They soon filled as more people heard that Jesus was in the city and learned of his whereabouts. Steven and the lamb continued to make record time moving in and out, over and under, which they did so well. Steven was moving on instinct. The familiar feeling in his stomach had reappeared once again, making him question his intentions and his motives. Even though he'd had the conversation a thousand times with himself, he found himself asking what he would say. Regardless of the crowd and his own uncertainty, Steven continued moving forward without hesitation.

Steven reached the palm tree in front of Sera's house. He looked through the gate at the huge wooden door and saw there was no one in the yard except Rosetta and a few workers who were all crying bitterly. Steven heard people laughing and looked around at the crowd of people that had gathered. Somehow, something seemed out of place. This didn't seem to be the atmosphere of the house where a young girl had just died.

"Is he here? Is Jesus here?" Steven asked a man who was standing in a nearby group talking.

The man looked at Steven and smiled. "Yes, he's here, but he's much too late," he replied.

"Why are people laughing?" asked Steven, becoming more upset.

"Well, the funny thing is that Jesus thinks we don't know what we see with our own eyes. He says the little girl isn't dead but asleep." All of the men in the group chuckled again.

"Are you sure she isn't asleep?" Steven replied, sounding even more upset at the accusations.

"Listen, young man," started one of the men in the group, but he was cut short by a cry from inside the house.

A hush fell over the crowd as the large wooden door of the house creaked open. Steven and the lamb made their way closer to the gate. The door opened, and Steven saw Jesus in the doorway holding Sera's hand! The crowd roared. Jesus smiled at Sera and gave her hand to her mother, who dropped to her knees, hugging the child. Jesus then turned directly toward Steven and the lamb.[13] Steven stood entranced as Jesus walked the short brick path to the gate. The noise from the crowd grew faint as Jesus approached. Steven saw Jesus's head lower, looking him right in the eyes. A smile formed on the corners of Jesus's mouth and in his eyes, and he nodded at Steven just like before at the temple in Jerusalem. Steven stood motionless, expressionless. Stepping aside, he just watched as Jesus walked past and disappeared into the crowd with his disciples.

Steven was snapped back to the noise and celebration only when he realized he was being hugged.

"Steven!" he heard Sera say. "I'm back! I feel terrific!" Sera took Steven by the hand and led him into the yard where her parents, Rosetta, and the other members of the house were huddled.

Rosetta immediately hugged Steven. "You were right, Steven. All along you were right. Jesus is the answer," she said, hugging Steven again. "Stay with us. I'm going to prepare a meal."

"I can't, Rosetta. I really should go. I should go catch up with Jesus," Steven said with disappointment as he looked out at the crowd of people in the street. "Valmus is on his way here. Maybe we can find him before he leaves the city."

"I understand," said Rosetta. "It's such a wonderful time."

Steven hugged Sera. "I'm so happy you feel better," he said to her.

"Thank you, Steven," she said. "Thank you for believing I could get better." Sera hugged Steven again, and he and the lamb walked out to the crowd in the street.

Steven and the lamb didn't leave Sera's house as quickly as they had arrived. Steven was disappointed but also puzzled with himself for not running to catch up with Jesus and talking to him like he had planned for so long.

He and the lamb made it back to the lower part of the city, and Steven was surprised he hadn't run into Valmus. He was almost home, and there were no crowds at the synagogue or in the street, making Steven believe Jesus had left the city. Steven walked down the street to his house and, noticing the horse out front from a distance, began to run.

The door was open, and he ran inside. "Dad!" he yelled with excitement.

"Steven, my boy," the familiar voice replied. Steven ran into the waiting arms of his father, and the two embraced each other.

"How are you?" his father asked.

"Good, good. It's been an exciting morning. Margaret is well. Sera is well. But he was right next to me, and I didn't talk to him.

"Steven, that's wonderful," his mother said. "About Margaret and Sera, I mean," she added.

"He looked at me and nodded just like before, but that's not talking. I didn't talk to him as I had planned."

"That's okay, Steven," his mother said, stepping forward and putting her hand on his shoulder. "There will be a time."

"And you never know what other business Jesus has at this time," continued his father. "I'm afraid there's more bad news." Steven and his mother looked at him. "Herod had John the Baptist put to death."[14]

CHAPTER NINETEEN

J esus and John the Baptist were related, you know," Isa said as Steven and his parents sat at the kitchen table having breakfast.

"That's right," his mother added. "Jesus's mother, Mary, and John's mother, Elizabeth, are relatives."

"That's probably why Jesus hasn't been back to Capernaum for so long," Steven said with a tone of deep discouragement. "I don't know why you won't let me go look for him. He's probably somewhere near the east shore."

"Yes, I heard he was over near Bethsaida," his father said.

"Steven, we've already been over that issue for weeks," his mother replied.

"But you let me go look for him by myself before."

"I let you go look for him alone when he was closer. Not near Bethsaida. And Sera desperately needed help. And—" Steven's mother started to continue when she noticed the lamb had jumped up and put his front feet on the edge of her chair and was looking up at her with big, innocent eyes.

"How desperate do we have to be?" Steven asked.

Steven's father smiled at her, raising his eyebrows.

"Oh, you two," his mother said as she slipped from her chair and walked to the kitchen.

"You know, I've got some time off."

Steven felt his back straighten involuntarily and his eyes look sideways at his father.

"We could go take a look in the hill country and be back in time to leave for the Passover Feast," his father continued.

Steven's posture continued to straighten as he looked over to his mother. The lamb jumped up into the chair where she had been sitting and perked it's ears with the new level of excitement that was rising in the room.

"Could we?" Steven asked, looking at his father, then his mother, and then back to his father.

Steven's parents locked eyes and communicated without words as adults often do. "I think that might be a good idea," Steven's mother finally said. "The three of you can spend some time together and give me some time to get a few things done here."

"Yahoo!" Steven shouted as he jumped up and ran to his mother and hugged her. "Thank you, Mom!" he said, squeezing her around the waist. "This will be great!" Steven then ran to his father and threw his arms around his neck. "Thanks, Dad! We can leave right away!" The lamb, which had both front feet on the table at this point, jumped to the floor and stood by Steven, who was hardly able to control his excitement. "I've got a bag packed with everything we need! We can leave right now! I'll get it!"

Steven and the lamb dashed from the kitchen toward the rear of the house in a flurry of energy and excitement. Isa and Martha smiled at each other.

"Well, looks like I'm going on a little adventure," Isa said as he rose and walked across the room.

"Well, looks like you are," Martha replied as the two embraced.

"Are you sure you don't want to go? It might be nice to visit home and see some family."

"Not this time," Martha said dreamily, lost in their embrace. "But do find Simon and Andrew. It's been so long since I've heard from those two."

"I will. I'm sure we'll see them," Isa replied.

A commotion of feet and little hooves came thundering from the rear of the house, and Steven and the lamb came sliding around the corner into the kitchen. "Come on! Let's go! Let's go! Let's go!" he said, scarcely able to control his excitement.

"All right, here we go," Steven's father replied. "Do you have your pack?" he asked Steven.

"You bet," Steven said, holding his bag high.

"Here, you can carry these parcels Mom made for us. This will be enough to get us there, and we'll pick up more for the trip home."

"Okay. Striker for a fire, wrap for sleeping at night, bread and fish for food—that's it. We're ready. Let's go."

"Hey, not so fast there, world traveler," his mother said, walking toward Steven and the lamb. "I can't let you get out of here without a hug." Steven hugged his mother deeply. "You be careful out there, and you watch after these two," she said, reaching down and scratching the lamb behind the ears.

"We'll be careful, Mom," Steven said.

Steven's parents hugged again, and Isa headed to the door. Steven and the lamb were already out of the house.

"Look. It's going to be a beautiful day. No storms this trip," Steven said, waving his arms as if displaying the clear morning sky. "It's going to be fantastic," he resounded as he and the lamb hurried down the street.

"Wait up there, partner!" Isa called and hurried after him.

"You're going to get left behind right at the start." Steven's mother laughed. "See you soon!" she yelled after them.

"Love you, dear." Steven's father turned and waved, and the three were off.

It was a perfect morning. The city was beginning to bustle, but roosters could still be heard. Steven and his father walked to the gate in record time. "Well, isn't this a fine-looking trio?"

Steven turned toward the familiar voice. "Valmus!"

"Now where would you fellows be headed on such a blessed morning?" Valmus asked as the three walked up.

Steven hugged Valmus. Isa shook hands with him, and they embraced. "We're going to find Jesus," Steven replied, full of excitement.

"I see. I see. And where are you going to begin your search?" Valmus quizzed him.

"Over at the east shore," Steven quickly replied. Steven felt the familiar feeling about to overwhelm and cause him to explain where they were going, how they were going to get there, everything they were taking, but he stopped and took a deep breath.

Valmus smiled and placed his right hand on Steven's shoulder. "That would be a wonderful place to start," he replied.

"Isn't it going to be a wonderful day?" Isa said as he looked around and smiled at the sun coming up.

"Indeed, indeed," Valmus replied. "I'm working now. Have you heard? I just can't seem to start my day without beginning at a gate. There are so many people who helped me. It seems I always find someone to help here."

"Valmus, that's wonderful." Isa shook Valmus's right hand and put his left on his shoulder. "We're both very lucky people."

Steven and the lamb had started out the gate. "Come on! Let's go!" Steven shouted as he and the lamb looked back at the two men.

"Looks like you're going to do well just keeping up today." Valmus laughed. "You two watch out for your dad!" he yelled after Steven.

"We will!" Steven called back. "See you soon!"

Isa waved goodbye to Valmus and then scurried to catch up with Steven and the lamb.

"We're not going to run all the way to the east shore, are we?" Steven's father asked in a joking voice. He caught up with Steven and the lamb and settled in with the pace they were walking.

"I feel like I could," Steven replied. "This is going to be so great."

Isa smiled as the three hurried down the road with the morning sun on their faces.

CHAPTER TWENTY

W e must be getting close. There are more people on the road," Steven said as he and his father walked. "Yes. This is the area where John said a lot of people were going, and your grandfather has a pretty good idea of what's going on around here," Isa replied. "Jesus shouldn't be hard to find. When John said a lot of people, I think he was talking about *a lot* of people," Steven's father continued.

Steven and his father started up a hill that was pretty much like every other hill they had walked up since arriving to that part of the country. Steven and the lamb hurried ahead, almost running.

"Where do you two get all that energy?" Steven's father called. Several people chuckled as they all made their way to the top. "That certainly is a beautiful lamb," he heard one woman remark. Isa noticed Steven and the lamb had stopped when they reached the top of the hill. He didn't find the fact that they had stopped unusual, but something was peculiar. Most of the time when Steven waited for him to catch up he was encouraging him up the hill or asking a question or making a comment about something. This time both Steven and the lamb had stopped dead in their tracks. No words of encouragement. No questions or comments. It was almost as if the road ended and there was nothing on the other side of the hill.

"Hey. What's up?" said Steven's father as he approached Steven and the lamb. "Wow!" he exclaimed as the view on the other side of the hill came into sight. "Looks like we've made it."

A sea of people were gathered in a basin between hills that somewhat resembled an amphitheater. Thousands upon thousands of men, women, and children were seated comfortably on the grassy slopes.

"Look at all these people. This must be the place. He must be here," were several of the comments heard from people in the group as they reached the top of the hill.

"How will we ever find him?" Steven asked, as if talking to himself.

"Well," his father replied, "We'll start on one side and make our way to the other, and surely we'll find him somewhere in between. Let's stay together, though. Something tells me we're not the only ones wanting to get close to Jesus today."

Steven and his father started down the hill toward the crowd of people. The road was clear as people continued to find open places on the hillside and made themselves comfortable.

Steven and his father were still somewhat mesmerized by the sheer size of the group of people as they began working their way to the other side. Isa noticed a strange contentment among the people. As they walked along through the crowd, everyone seemed happy. They were calmly, quietly resting as if something were about to happen.

"You won't find a place any closer," an old woman called as they walked past. "You might as well find a spot and be comfortable," she said.

Steven and his father stopped and acknowledged the old woman. Isa smiled and nodded. "But I've got to talk to Jesus," Steven replied. "Have you seen him?"

"What a beautiful lamb," the woman said. "Oh, yes. He's here," she continued. "He says such wonderful things and does such wonderful things. But you don't have to see him to hear him. When he speaks, everyone here can hear him just like he's right next to them. It's wonderful."

"That's nice," Steven said. "But I've got to talk to him."

"He's there," the old woman said, pointing to the hill on the other side of the crowd. "Good luck. It's really crowded there." Steven and his father bid the old woman farewell and continued through the crowd toward the hill.

"Hurry and find a spot!" she called after them. "It will be time to eat soon."

At first there was still sitting room, but as they neared the other side, it became standing room only. "I wonder what she was talking about?" Steven asked as the three walked along.

"What's that?" his father replied.

"She said it was going to be time to eat soon. I can't tell that these people brought anything. And those who did won't have enough to share."

"I'm not sure. This all seems out of the ordinary to me, but we're getting closer," his father said. "Stay together."

They worked their way through the people and soon came to a place where the crowd stopped. Men were standing in a circle making room for a small group with Jesus in the middle. Steven was holding the lamb in his arms and saw Jesus move his head to see around the people he was talking to and notice his arrival. Immediately, Steven saw his uncle Andrew turn from the group of men talking to Jesus and walk toward him and his father.

"Isa, Steven, what are you two doing here?" Andrew said.

With this greeting and recognition from Andrew, Steven and his father stepped into the inner circle where it was not so crowded.

"Well, it appears this is where all the excitement is," Isa replied.

"Is Martha with you?" Andrew asked.

"No. She didn't come. It's just us boys this trip," Isa said.

"We just stayed at Grandma and Grandpa's," Steven said without his eyes ever leaving the men at the center of the circle.

"Oh, good, good. They're all right I suppose?" Andrew asked.

Isa nodded with an affirmative smile.

"Tell them I said hello on your way back. Isa, there is so much to know, so much to hear. I truly believe Jesus is the Messiah. The one we've been waiting for all this time. But we have a bit of a problem now," Andrew said.

"What's wrong?" Isa asked.

"All these people. They've come here because of all the miraculous signs Jesus performs on the sick but brought nothing with them. They came from all over. I'm not sure how they even made it out here. Many came to hear Jesus's teaching, but many need healing, and they have nothing. Jesus has asked us where we will buy bread. Do you think there would be enough to share?"

Isa's eyes widened a little. "I don't know, Andrew. This is a lot of people," he said.

"Steven, do you have any of the food parcels your mother makes?" Andrew asked.

"Yes. We have a few more," Steven said, looking in his bag and handing his uncle a wrapped parcel of food.

"Good," said Andrew. "I'll be right back."

Andrew walked back to the group of men standing around Jesus. In a few minutes the group of men went into the crowd and began asking everyone to sit down. When those who had been standing were resting comfortably on the grassy slopes of the hill, Jesus stood with a small basket containing the loaves and fish. Jesus bowed his head and gave thanks and then walked straight to Steven and handed him some of the food. As he did, Jesus smiled and nodded his head just as he had done the times before. Jesus then handed food to Isa, and then the people next to him, and the people next to them. Steven and his father watched in amazement as Jesus and his helpers quickly distributed food to everyone who was present.[15]

Soon Jesus was out of sight, and everyone was quietly visiting and enjoying their meal. Andrew and Simon came back to Steven and Isa and sat with them.

"How is this possible?" Isa asked.

"Things are constantly happening that we don't understand. Jesus always gives the honor and glory to God the Father," Simon said.

"I need to talk to Jesus," Steven said. "But every time I get close or have a chance, I get scared or something happens, and I don't."

"Don't worry," Andrew said. "There will be a time, and isn't this a feisty little fellow?" he continued, recognizing the lamb that had jumped in between them and began pushing on Andrew's leg with his head.

They all laughed at the lamb. "It's so wonderful just being around him," Simon continued. "One thing we've learned is that things are happening just the way they're supposed to. Andrew's right. There will be a time for you to talk to Jesus, but this probably isn't it."

"Why's that?" Steven asked.

"People are recognizing Jesus because of all the miraculous signs," Andrew said.

"People aren't fully realizing who Jesus is, the Son of the living God, but think he is a prophet who has come into the world. They're talking of making him king, even if by force," Simon said.

"There is talk of this here. Today," Andrew said.

"Jesus has withdrawn to a mountain where the crowd will not go. The crowd will disperse, and then Jesus will return. We'll go to meet him. Is there something we could talk to Jesus about for you?" Simon asked.

Steven looked at his father, who put his hand on his shoulder. "No," Steven said, "this is something I need to do. Thanks, though."

Steven rubbed the lamb that enjoyed being the center of attention as the men talked. "The Passover Feast is coming soon," Isa said. "I'm sure there will be a chance to talk to Jesus there."

"Probably so," Simon said.

"Don't worry," Andrew continued. "I'm sure everything will happen just right."

Steven made his best attempt to smile and nod.

"Are you stopping by Mom and Dad's on the way back?" Simon asked.

"Yes, we are," Isa replied.

"If you would, be sure and tell them we love them," he said.

"It's been a while since we've seen them or Martha," Andrew added. "Be sure and give our love to her when you get home."

"We will," Steven's father assured him. "And we look forward to seeing you in Jerusalem." The men stood and embraced, and then Simon and Andrew began helping other men gather the leftover pieces of bread and fish.

Steven and his father looked at each other, and the lamb looked up. "I'll race you home," Steven's father said.

Steven smiled and replied, "You're on," and the three headed back toward Bethsaida.

CHAPTER TWENTY-ONE

O h, my love," Isa said as he and Martha embraced one another.

Steven and the lamb bustled into the house behind his father. "You should have seen all the people!" he exclaimed, walking alongside his mother as she knelt down and embraced him. "And five barley loaves and two small fish fed everyone with plenty to spare," he continued.

"Oh, I can't imagine," his mother replied, looking at Isa, who smiled and nodded his head. "It sounds like quite a trip," she said. "And good job, little lamb. I knew you'd bring them back safe and sound."

The lamb jumped up with its front feet on her knee as Steven's mother rubbed the side of its head.

Martha stood and put a hand on each of their shoulders. "I'm sure glad you're home, but it looks like this will be a short stay. They've come by several times looking for you. They wouldn't say much, but they want you to go to Jericho before the feast."

"Well, so much for time off." Isa laughed. "There's so much talk about Jesus, and there's just not enough messengers."

"Let's get a bite to eat, and then you can go to the synagogue and see what they say," Steven's mother said.

"Hopefully we can leave in the morning," Isa replied.

"Or tonight," Steven said. Laughing, the three went to the kitchen.

Steven and the lamb ran to the front door when he heard his father return from the synagogue. "Are we leaving? Are we going tonight or tomorrow? Is it important?" It was very clear that Steven was ready to leave, that very moment, if need be.

"Well, yes and no," Steven's father replied. Martha had joined them from the kitchen at this point and was wiping her hands with a towel. "Yes, it's important we get to Jericho as soon as we can, but no, we're not leaving tonight. Arrangements have been made for us to take a cart so we can all go because of the feast."

"That's sure good of them to let us travel together," Steven's mother replied.

"I'll say. I sure won't mind riding after that walk we were just on. How about you?" Steven's father asked, looking to Steven and the lamb.

"We could run to Jericho," Steven said, turning and running toward his room. "We could leave tonight, but there's a few things to get ready first."

Isa shrugged his shoulders. "I'm surprised I'm not running," he said as he and Martha walked to the kitchen. "And I'm surprised we're not leaving tonight. They've been sending messengers out as soon as they've arrived. There's an incredible amount of anxiety among the leaders, and all of that anxiety is focused on Jesus."

"I don't understand why they can't focus on the miracles and the good that's being done," Martha said.

"It's not that easy," Isa said. "There's a lot involved, but it's not looking good. A cart is to be here at daylight. We should get some rest." The two sat quietly in the kitchen holding hands and staring at the table.

CHAPTER TWENTY-TWO

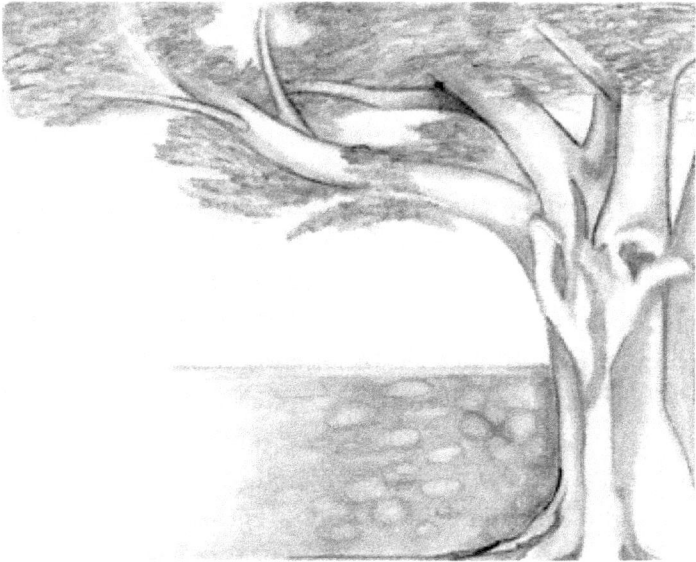

I t was a beautiful time of year. The temperature was cool, and the weather was perfect.

"We're getting very close," Steven said. Steven held on to his father's shoulders as he and the lamb stood in the cart looking down the road.

"Yes, I believe you're right. We should be in Jericho shortly," Steven's father said.

"It's just beautiful here." Steven's mother said. "I've always loved Jericho. There's something sort of magical about this place.

"True," Isa added with a chuckle. "Do you suppose it was a day just like today when Joshua and the Israelites marched around the walls of Jericho?"

"I remember," Steven said. "On the seventh day, the seventh trip around the wall, the trumpet blew, the people shouted, and the walls of Jericho fell."[16]

"Right," Steven's mother said. "That's the story."

"There sure seems to be a lot of people," Steven said.

"That's true," his father replied. "I know it's time for the feast, but seems like most people pass through farther west."

"Maybe Jesus is here," Steven said with a tone of anticipation.

"Maybe so," Steven's mother said. "Something is definitely going on. I suppose Chloe will know what's happening."

"Yes, we'll be at her house soon," Isa said.

The cart rolled to the top of the hill, and Jericho was in sight. The road ahead was growing more and more congested, and people moved out of the way when they heard the sound of the cart's wheels on the rocky road.

By the time Steven and his family arrived at Jericho, the city was full to overflowing with people.

"This is almost like the feast has been moved to Jericho." Isa laughed. "I don't think I've ever seen this many people here at one time."

"It's got to be Jesus," Steven said. "Remember all the people out on the hillside?"

Isa guided the cart down a small street of quaint little dwellings. They stopped at one about halfway down the street.

"Aunt Chloe, we're here!" Steven shouted as he and the lamb piled out of the back of the cart.

Isa was helping Martha down from the cart when they heard a woman's voice. "Oh, you *are* here. Hello, Steven."

"Hello, Aunt Chloe," Steven said as he and the lamb rushed to the woman and hugged her. Isa and Martha were close behind. "And who is this?" Steven's aunt asked as she knelt down to examine the lamb, which seemed to puff and strike a pose at the attention.

"This is my lamb," Steven said matter-of-factly. "I got him at the temple. I talked to Jesus. Well, sort of."

"Yes. I've heard. Your uncle Andrew has told me this story. It sounds like a grand adventure," she said as she and Steven's mother embraced and greeted one another.

"So you've seen Andrew?" Martha asked. She was answered only with a smile.

"Hello, Isa. Come have something to drink."

"Thanks, Chloe. How are you?" Steven's father replied. "And what's going on in Jericho?"

"Haven't you heard?" Isa's sister chuckled. "I thought you were in the loop on everything that was going on with Jesus."

"Well," Isa said, "I do know a few things that are coming from the synagogues, but it would be impossible to keep up with everything Jesus is doing, what people are saying about him, and where he's going to be. Why?"

"Why, Aunt Chloe? Is he coming here?" Steven asked. The rise of his anticipation was growing more evident with each moment.

"That's what I've heard. They say Jesus has left the hill country and is going to pass through Jericho on his way to the feast."

"That makes sense," Steven's father said. "I've never seen so many people in Jericho at one time."

"That's awesome!" Steven yelled. "You were right all along, Dad. It's going to work out just right," Steven said, hugging his father rather nervously.

Steven's mother noticed his anxiety and put her hand on his shoulder to reassure him. "This might just be the time, Steven. You must be careful, though. You're not as familiar with Jericho as you are other places," she said.

"And isn't that a shame!" Chloe chided, mussing Steven's hair and then patting Isa on the cheek. "All this traveling back and forth and to and fro, it seems like we'd see more of you," she said, laughing.

"Oh, Chloe." Martha laughed as Chloe threw her arm around her shoulder and headed inside.

"Have fun, Steven!" his aunt called back.

"Be careful!" his mother shouted, looking over her shoulder.

Steven and his father were left looking at each other. "Be careful, Steven," his father said, smiling.

"I will," Steven said meekly. "Do you think he's really coming?"

"He could be. We did just see him in the hill country."

"Will you go with me?" Steven asked.

"I'd love to, partner," Steven's father said, "but I've got to go by the synagogue first, and I'm not sure how long that will take. You know I've got to wait sometimes, and with all this excitement, it might be a while."

"I know," Steven said as the three headed back down the street the way they had come.

"Steven, you'll be fine," his father said, pulling him close as they walked. The noise from the street ahead was growing. Steven's father smiled and pulled him close again. "You'll be fine."

"Yeah. Okay," Steven said as they walked. "I'll meet you at the synagogue."

Steven's father looked down and smiled. Steven looked straight ahead as he and the lamb walked with his father. Running didn't even cross Steven's mind.

As they reached the end of the street, the noise and the excitement of the crowd became very evident.

"Boy!" Steven's father said. "There's definitely something happening here today."

"Can you stay with me for a while?" Steven asked. The three stopped behind a wall of people that lined the street. "Just for a while until we see what's going on?"

"Steven, I'd love to. Something really exciting must be in the works, but I've got to get over to the synagogue. Why don't you do this? You and the lamb work your way around and see if you can find out what's happening. I'll go straight to the synagogue and take care of some business, and by the time the two of you get there, I'll be finished, and we'll come back together. How about that?"

Isa had his hand on Steven's shoulder at this point, and Steven was looking at the ground.

"Hey, this isn't like you. What's up?" Steven's father asked.

"I don't know. Any other time this would be great, but something just seems weird. I mean, I want to talk to Jesus, but sometimes I don't know what I'll say when I find him."

Isa laughed out loud and hugged Steven close. "Don't worry, Steven. Things will happen just the way they're supposed to. Has God ever let you down before?" he asked.

"I don't guess so," Steven replied.

"No. So why would he this time? Try to relax, and remember God has everything under control."

Steven made an attempt at smiling. "Okay. Everything will happen just the way it's supposed to."

"That-a-boy," Steven's father said. "Now find out what's happening, and I'll see you two at the synagogue."

"All right," Steven said. "We'll see you in a little while."

Steven's father smiled and then disappeared into the crowd.

Steven looked down at the lamb with a look of bewilderment. "Well, where do you think we should start?" he asked the lamb while rubbing its head and ears. "What's that? You think we should just ask someone?" Steven was smiling now. "Well, let's find someone to ask," Steven said, and he and the lamb began walking behind the crowd of people along the street.

Finding someone to ask wasn't the problem. The street was lined with people, crowded with people as if a parade were about to begin. But this was obviously no normal parade. It was as if the whole city of Jericho had showed up and crowded into this one street. Some people were laughing and having fun, and others seemed angry and were pushing their way closer.

"This is way too crowded here," Steven said to the lamb. "Let's head farther up the street and see if we can find some steps or a wall to get on.

"They walked a little farther, but things weren't any different. The street was extremely crowded, and people were working to get into any kind of position to see. There was chanting coming from down the street; so, whatever it was, it was getting close.

Steven was getting very excited now. He and the lamb were continuing to make their way down the street behind the crowd. Suddenly someone pushed, what seemed to be a child, away from the people crowding the street. The small person sailed right into Steven, knocking him to the ground! "You get back! You don't deserve to be up here!" the man from the crowd yelled back.

It was so fast Steven wasn't sure what had happened. Steven sat up, and the lamb was right there as if checking to see that he was all right. The two watched as the person who was pushed into him rolled around and finally made it to a sitting position. But it wasn't a boy; it was a man. A very short man.

Steven and the man sat looking at each other for a moment and then started to get up.

"Sorry about that," the man said as he pushed the ground, getting his knees under himself.

"Sorry. Yep, I should have known better than to try to get too close," he said, pushing on his knee.

"What was that all about?" Steven asked as he took the man by the arm and helped him to his feet.

"They hate me," the little man said, dusting himself off.

"Who hates you?" asked Steven, turning his attention back to the noise and chanting of the crowd.

"All of them. They all hate me," the man said again. "I've got my job, and they've got theirs. Well, some of them have jobs, and they all hate me."

"Listen!" Steven said excitedly, almost interrupting the man. "I've heard that before. It's Jesus! They're calling him King of Israel!"

"Of course it's Jesus," the little man said. "This was my chance to see him, and now I won't be able to."

"We'll see him!" Steven said. "Everything happens just the way it's supposed to! Come on."

"Well, I don't know about—"

"Come on!" Steven shouted back, and he and the lamb were off at lightning speed. The street ended in a square along with several other streets. In the center there was a fountain and sycamore-fig trees. Steven looked back, and the little man was hurrying but seemed to be making more sideways movement than forward. When he finally caught up with Steven, he leaned over and put his hands on his knees. Steven thought he looked like he was going to go back down on one knee.

"Whoa, there, mister! We're not there yet," Steven said.

"You know," the little man gasped, "I think I might have gone just about as far as I can go."

"Nonsense!" Steven exclaimed. "Listen. He's almost here!"

"Well, how much farther are you thinking of going?" he asked, standing up straight.

"About ten feet," Steven replied.

"Ten feet!" said the man, looking around. "What good could that possibly do?"

Steven looked up into the tree they were standing beside, and the people around them by the road began calling, "King of Israel!"

"You can do it!" Steven cried over the crowd.

"Son, do you know how long it's been since I've climbed a tree? I'll break my neck!" he laughed.

"Come on!" Steven cried again. "We'll help you. Once you're on the first limb, you've got it made. It's like a ladder."

Steven cupped his hands together and put them on his knee to help the man up on the first limb of the tree.

"Okay," the man said with a nervous smile. "We can do this." He stepped into Steven's hands and pulled on the tree limb.

Steven lifted, and the lamb pushed with his head, and finally they had the man standing on the first limb. After that, the little man seemed to gain confidence and went up two more limbs, where he could easily see over the heads of the people standing along the street. He looked down and smiled at Steven, raised one hand, and then quickly reestablished his grip.

Suddenly, the people on the street stopped calling. The crowd parted, and Jesus walked right up to the tree. Jesus looked at Steven and smiled and then up at the little man and said, "Zacchaeus, come down immediately. I must stay at your house today."[17]

The little man started down immediately, and some of the men who were with Jesus helped him to the ground. "Yes. Yes, sir. I was so hoping to get to see you today. There are so many things I would like to ask you. Come. Come to my house. It's this way."

The little man turned to leave, but stopped in his tracks. He turned back to Steven and took Steven's hand in his. "Thank you, son. Thank you," he said, and then turned and left.

Jesus looked at Steven and nodded just as he had the times before and then he and his disciples followed the man. The crowd murmured as Jesus left. Steven heard someone say the word *sinner*. He watched as Jesus and the little man walked away, and Jesus's disciples filed by.

"Hey, Steven." Steven didn't hear his uncle at first.

"Hey, Steven," Andrew said, getting Steven's attention by cupping his rough hand behind Steven's neck. "Imagine seeing you here."

"Yeah," was all Steven could reply.

"I suppose your dad's at the synagogue. Did your mom come this trip or did she go on to May's?"

"She's here," Steven replied. "She's at Aunt Chloe's."

"Great!" Andrew replied. "I was planning on trying to get by there myself. Maybe I'll see you there. If not, we'll all be together in Jerusalem." Andrew smiled and waved, then turned to catch up with the others.

All Steven could do was nod his head and watch as they all walked out of sight.

The crowd began to break up, and people talked quietly in small groups, which quickly disbursed. Steven looked in the direction Jesus and the others had left until he felt the lamb brush against his leg. Steven looked down without changing his expression, and then slowly began walking in Jesus's footsteps.

Steven walked as if in a daze. He was aware of what was going on around him but not really concerned. Almost like his feelings. He was aware he had missed another opportunity to talk to Jesus, but it didn't seem to concern him. Not as much as he thought it would have. Thoughts flooded Steven's mind; he was emotionless, but not completely unfeeling. He wondered about the little man and had a good feeling that he got to talk to Jesus. As Steven walked, he was completely oblivious to his father, who was rushing toward him. "Hey, Steven. There you are. Did you see him? Did you talk to him?"

Steven just shook his head. "I did see Jesus. And we sort of talked. I didn't get to ask him about the lamb, though."

Steven's father was hurrying. Steven remained calm and unhurried. "Well, that's okay," his father said, hurrying out ahead of Steven and the lamb, waving his arms for them to catch up. "I'm sure Jesus will be in Jerusalem while we're there, and you'll get another chance."

Steven's father continued to motion toward Steven for him to hurry with him. The lamb had gotten the idea and jumped ahead in between Steven and his father, looking back. Steven was still calm and collected, as if deep in thought.

"Speaking of Jerusalem," his father said, "I've got to get there in a hurry. Right now. You know what I mean."

Steven looked at his father, who was considerably ahead of him at this point, and the lamb that was bouncing back and forth between them. Steven came to, as if waking up. "Okay," he said, running to catch up with his father. His father gave him a pat on the back, and the three hurried back toward his aunt's house.

"Hello, hello!" his father yelled as they ran into the house.

"We're in here!" Steven heard his mother and aunt shout back in unison and then laugh.

Steven, his father, and the lamb came crashing into the kitchen. "All this rush doesn't look like a good sign," Martha reported.

"We've got to leave," Isa said.

"Immediately?" Steven's mother and her sister-in-law asked in unison, laughing even more than before.

"Immediately," Isa said, cutting their laughter short.

"Well, what must be, must be." Chloe sighed. "It must be a very important message."

"It's amazing. Have you heard of the man named Lazarus?" Steven's father asked, almost as excited as Steven got at times. "He was dead. Not sick or lame or blind. Dead! In the tomb. For three days!" his father continued. "And Jesus brought him back to life!" Steven's father stood wide eyed, beaming at the others. "It's amazing."[18]

"That is amazing," Chloe said very seriously.

"That's why there are so many people," Martha added.

"No one could do the things Jesus does if God weren't with him," Isa said.

"I don't know why the leaders can't see these miraculous signs as good and beneficial. It's almost as if they're discouraged. They say the whole world has gone after him," Martha said. "I'm sorry it was such a short visit," she said taking Chloe by the hand.

"And that they keep messengers hopping from one place to the next," Chloe said. "We'll see each other in Jerusalem in a few days. We'll meet at May's house."

"Steven, did you see Simon and Andrew with Jesus this afternoon?" his mother asked.

"Yes. Uncle Andrew said he was going to try to come by here, but if he didn't see us here he'd meet us in Jerusalem."

Steven's mother and aunt exchanged smiles.

"Well, there you go," Steven's father said. "Sounds like a family reunion in Jerusalem." At this, he headed to the door and looked back as a sign for the others to follow.

Steven's mother and aunt hugged each other and headed outside. His aunt laughed when she saw the lamb push Steven as he climbed up the wheel of the cart. "Now, you two make quite a team," she said.

"That's what they say," Steven replied.

They all said their farewells, and the cart was soon creaking down the street.

"Bringing a dead man back to life," Steven's mother said quietly. "If people hadn't paid attention to Jesus before, they'll have to now."

"I'm not sure it's going to achieve the desired response from everyone," Isa said. "It sounds like some people are pretty upset."

Steven and the lamb nestled into the bags and were soon fast asleep. The rocking and creaking of the cart bathed over them as they headed south to Jerusalem.

CHAPTER
TWENTY-THREE

S teven's father was already gone when he woke, which was early.

"Mom, we're leaving!" Steven called to his mother.

"Wait just a minute. You need something to eat. No telling how long you'll be out there today," she said, appearing from the kitchen with a smile.

Steven and the lamb hurried through their breakfast and were ready to go.

"I guess you won't mind delivering these while you're making your rounds, will you?" his aunt May asked, handing Steven a wrap containing small parcels of food.

"And I know they're busy, but if you see your uncles, tell them a short visit would be much appreciated," Steven's mother added, with the other two women agreeing.

"I will," Steven replied, walking toward the door with his mother following.

"I love you, Steven," his mother said, kneeling to give him a hug. "I love you too, you furry, little fellow," she said, rubbing the lamb on the head.

"Love you, Mom," Steven said.

"I know you'll be careful, but the city is very crowded," she said.

"I will," he replied. Steven was emotionless.

"Hey," Steven's mother called as he headed out the door. "Keep your spirits up. You never know what the day may bring," she said, smiling, raising her hand to wave goodbye.

"Thanks, Mom!" Steven called back, waving with one hand and holding the wrap of food over his shoulder with the other.

Jerusalem was different. Things looked relatively the same, but somehow everything seemed different. Steven headed up the street toward the temple. The city was extremely crowded. People from all over the region were gathered for the Passover Feast, and the name of Jesus was in the air. People everywhere were talking about the wonderful things he was doing and teaching. Everyone but the leaders.

Even though people were everywhere, Steven made it to the back entrance of the temple without seeing anyone he knew. As he rounded a corner and headed up the steps to the out-of-the-way entrance, he heard someone shout, "Hey, messenger boy!"

Steven looked down and saw Judi and about ten other boys hurrying up the street to the narrow steps.

"I figured I'd see you sooner or later." Judi sneered.

"Not if I see you first," Steven called back as he and the lamb continued their ascent.

"You can run, little lamb, but you can't hide!" Judi yelled. "And don't even think that Jesus fellow gave him to you," Judi said, reaching the bottom of the steps. "It wasn't his to give. That lamb belongs to my father."

"This lamb belongs to God. Along with everything else!" Steven shouted back.

"Well, that's what I'm thinking." Judi laughed. "Let's give this lamb back to God."

Steven and the lamb ran inside and began running through the maze of rooms and walls in the back of the temple area. It was as if Steven was on autopilot. He ran without thinking where he was going, but his mind knew it was the right way.

"It's not over!" Steven heard Judi's voice echo through the corridors as he disappeared into the temple. "My father will put an end to this! All of this!"

As if running out of a cave, Steven ran into the open courtyard of the temple. The courtyards were crowded with people. Steven and the lamb worked their way among the crowd, but he didn't see anyone he knew until they got to the front steps leading out of the temple. Maundi was in the street below greeting people and telling them about how he couldn't walk for so long and the wonderful thing Jesus had done for him.

"Steven!" Maundi shouted when he saw Steven and the lamb approaching. "It's been a long time!" he said excitedly, throwing his arms around Steven with a warm greeting.

"You look great, Maundi. It's good to see you," Steven said. "And you're up. How are your knees?"

Maundi jumped and clicked his heels together. "As good as new," he replied.

"That's wonderful, Maundi," Steven said. "I thought the leaders told you to keep a low profile, though."

"Oh, they did. And I did. But you know, Steven, the more open I am, the less it seems they can do to me. And I've got to tell people the good news: there's finally someone from God who can help. People have to know. And I've got to be doing the right thing," he said with a smile. "The leaders don't like it, but somehow I'm still avoiding any unfortunate accidents."

"That's what we're trying to avoid this morning," Steven said, looking back. "Judi and his bunch are right behind us."

"I think he's coming," Maundi said with the same excitement as before.

Steven's face grew puzzled and concerned at Maundi's emotion. "Judi? Where?" he asked, looking through the crowd.

"No, not Judi. Jesus!" Maundi exclaimed. "I heard he was coming into the city this morning."

"That's wonderful, Maundi," Steven said. "Did you hear where?"

"The northeast gate. Come on. I'll go with you. I try not to stay in one spot too long anyway, no matter how good my luck is running," he said with a smile. "Don't test the Lord, right?"

Steven thought about what Maundi had said as they walked out of the inner city toward the northeast gate. 'Don't test the Lord.' Steven hoped he had not been testing God by not taking the opportunity to ask Jesus about the lamb, but the opportunity just never seemed right. Besides, if things were happening just the way they were supposed to, everything was just fine. Steven made it a point to completely avoid the topic while talking with Maundi.

"Have you seen Azack or the widow Mireb?" Steven asked.

"Yes. They're fine," Maundi replied. "They would love to see you, I'm sure. We may see them at the gate," Maundi continued. "From what I understand, it has become quite a procession wherever Jesus goes."

"I know what you mean." Steven went on to tell Maundi about the thousands of people near Bethsaida, about Jericho, and the short little man and the tree.

When they reached the gate, there were several carts loaded down with palm branches. Men were handing them out to people as they went out to meet Jesus.

As Steven, the lamb, and Maundi went out of the gate, a great crowd of people lined the street similar to what Steven had seen in Jericho. They could hear people talking about Lazarus, the man Jesus brought back to life. Soon they could hear people shouting, "Hosanna!" "Blessed is he who comes in the name of the Lord!" and, "Blessed be the King of Israel."[19]

Jesus was riding on a small donkey, and people laid the palm branches on the ground as he rode by.

"I bet he's going straight to the temple," Maundi said. "I think we should head over there. I really feel like something great is going to happen here in Jerusalem, and I want be right there to see it."

"Anything's possible," Steven agreed as the huge crowd consolidated and moved back inside the gate. Once back on the inside, the crowd dispersed. Many people did seem to be headed back the same direction as Maundi, Steven, and the lamb. As the crowd pressed through the street toward the temple, Steven noticed an old woman standing by a corner building with her hand out.

"There's the widow Mireb!" Steven said, making his way to the side.

"Steven!" she said. "It's so good to see you." She hugged him close. "And your little friend seems to be doing fine."

"Thanks," Maundi replied, winking at Steven.

"Oh, Maundi, I wasn't meaning you," she said as they all laughed together.

"How have you been doing?" Steven asked the woman as he untied the wrap of parcels.

"Pretty good, I suppose," she said. "If it wasn't for your family, Steven—"

"You know we're glad to help," Steven interrupted, handing the widow a small parcel of food. "And you know we're here anytime we can be."

"Thank you, Steven. Thank your whole family."

"Could you use two parcels?" Steven asked the widow.

"Well, if you could spare another, yes," she replied. "Jesus is here, and I have nothing to put into the church treasury."

"Oh, Mireb," Maundi said. "Don't make it sound like Jesus is just concerned with the temple treasury," he continued.

"That may be true, Maundi," the old woman shot back. "But we should all do our part."

Steven and the lamb watched the two older people interacting somewhat like children. He quietly handed her another small wrap of food.

"Thank you, Steven. I can sell this for two copper coins and at least have something to put in," she said, touching Steven's face with the palm of her hand.[20]

"Well, you might as well go with us, Mireb," Maundi said.

"Listen," Steven said, "you two take your time. I think we'll go back home for a bit. I think Dad's going to be home this afternoon. I don't know why, but I feel like I need to talk to him."

"Okay, Steven," Maundi said.

"We'll meet you at the temple in a little while," the widow Mireb said. "Thank you again."

"Here, Maundi," Steven said, handing him the wrap of parcels. "You may see others on your way back to the temple. I'll see you soon."

At this, Steven and the lamb were off toward his aunt's house. It didn't take them long to make the short distance. Steven opened the door and went inside. Once inside, he heard his father's voice coming from the kitchen.

"They said it was most important for me to take the message to Mindab, even though he was at an important meeting at Caiaphas's palace," Steven heard him say. "When I got to the palace, they told me to go on upstairs, and I couldn't believe what I heard," he continued. "They're planning to arrest him and kill him for no reason!" his father said in a hushed voice. "I couldn't believe it. They said they could get people to testify. I'm lucky I made it out of there. If they would have known I'd overheard—"

"We have to do something!" Steven exclaimed. The four adults in the kitchen jumped simultaneously. "We have to let him know! He's here in the city, and he must leave right away!" Steven's voice was panicked. His mother rose immediately and went to comfort the boy.

Steven backed away from his mother. "We have to do something right away!" he exclaimed again.

"Steven," his mother said calmly, "let's talk about this."

"There's no time! He's here in Jerusalem. I saw him come into the city this morning."

"I heard he was on his way here," Steven's father said.

The adults looked at each other, and Steven looked at the adults.

"What exactly can we do?" Steven's aunt asked. "We're dealing with powers beyond our control."

"We have to let him know. He has to leave now. I must tell Jesus before they get him. Maundi said he was going to the temple." Steven moved toward the door.

"Steven," his mother said again calmly, "let's talk before doing something rash."

"There's no time. They might try to get him at the temple." Steven ran to the door, threw it open, and ran into the street. "I'll be back and let you know what happens!" he yelled.

"Steven!" This time his mother's voice was anything but calm, but Steven and the lamb were gone.

"Steven!" she shouted again from outside the door. "Isa, find him!" she said, turning to her husband.

"I will, dear. I'll find him. He'll go straight to the temple, and I know just which way he'll go," Steven's father said, backing down the street in the direction Steven had gone. "We'll both be back soon," he said to the three women and then turned and hurried down the street.

The streets of Jerusalem were more crowded than Steven had ever seen them. People were everywhere. It was like a celebration bigger than the feast that had just occurred. Steven and the lamb worked through the crowds of people like air. They were in and out and around. Nothing slowed them down.

Steven reached the temple and ran up all the steps to the temple courtyard. He expected to find the temple crowded and people quietly listening to Jesus speak, but there was no sign of Jesus anywhere. He ran from one side of the courtyard to the other. No one was teaching or reading at all. Steven ran to the huge horns where people threw their offering to the temple treasury, and he saw Maundi and widow Mireb.

"Is Jesus here?" he asked, out of breath and with no greeting at all.

"Hi, Steven," Maundi said. "He was just here."

"I've got to find him now," Steven said.

Maundi and the widow smiled at each other. "I know, Steven. We must ask him about this lamb," Maundi said.

"It's important. It's a matter of life and death," Steven said, still panting.

"Is Judi still bothering you, Steven? We should go to his father and put a stop to that," the widow Mireb said angrily.

"No. It's not Judi. Maundi, where do you think he went? Surely he's still here in the city," Steven said.

"Steven, I'm not sure," Maundi said, growing more concerned with Steven and his behavior. "I heard he and his disciples were staying out at Gethsemane, but you're right.

He was just here. He probably went to find a quieter place to teach. Surely he's still here in the city."

"I've got to find him," Steven said again. "I'll check back." He and the lamb were off again.

Maundi and the widow Mireb looked at each other. "I wonder what that was all about," the widow said.

"I'm not sure," Maundi replied.

Just as suddenly as before, Steven's father appeared to the two. "Hello, Maundi. Mireb. Have you seen Steven?" he asked.

"You missed him by minutes," Maundi replied.

"Is everything okay?" the widow asked.

"Steven did seem a lot more wound up than usual," Maundi added.

"Yes. Well, I hope so, Mireb," he said. "I really need to find Steven. He's quite upset."

"He seemed to have the same sense of urgency about finding Jesus. And he was…quite upset," Maundi replied as if reasoning with himself.

"Steven said he was going to look for Jesus here in the city?" The statement the widow Mireb made came out like a question.

Steven's father turned his whole focus to her with his eyebrows raised, prodding for more information.

"Well," she continued, "Maundi did mention he heard Jesus and his disciples were staying at the garden of Gethsemane, probably because it's so secluded from the crowds, but he also said Jesus was still here in Jerusalem. He probably went to find a quieter place by the pools to teach. You know how he speaks of such wonderful things like life and water," she said, trying to sound encouraging. "Steven said he would come back here."

"You two stay here at the temple. Please." The urgency was clear in Isa's voice. "If you see Steven, tell him I said to stay with you until I get back here."

Both elderly people agreed they would keep watch at the temple until Isa returned.

Isa raced from the temple. He felt hot and had a lump in his throat that made it hard to swallow. Evening was getting closer. He knew Steven was a smart boy, but he also knew he was very upset, and the east hills were no place for a boy and a lamb to be alone at night.

CHAPTER
TWENTY-FOUR

S teven looked everywhere. Jerusalem was still crowded with people, but Jesus was nowhere to be found. Gethsemane. The name kept ringing in Steven's mind. He probably left and went there where it was quiet. He knew what he had to do. He knew what he should do. His parents would be worried. They would not approve, but there was no time to reason.

Before he realized it, Steven was staring at the northeast gate and the road that led to the east hills and Gethsemane. He and the lamb stood quietly before the gate with a beautiful sunset to their left.

There were still a few people coming and going through the gate. Voices kept running through Steven's mind as he contemplated what he and the lamb were about to do. *Everything happens just the way it's supposed to. Has God ever let you down before? Stay with people on the road.* And there were still people.

Steven began to walk slowly to the gate. King David wouldn't have been scared. He was just a boy, and he did great things. Steven's pace quickened. He would stay with the people. His parents would understand. His uncles were there. He had to do this.

By the time Steven and the lamb reached the gate, they were at a full run. People watched as they raced down the road toward the east hills. Steven didn't stop to talk. He didn't listen to what people were saying. He only had one thing on his mind: get to Gethsemane *fast*. At first, there seemed to be a lot of people still on the road. Steven and the lamb ran and didn't slow down. They ran from group to group, person to person, and soon found themselves alone. Softly the shades of evening were falling around them, but they were close now. Soon he and the lamb would be with Jesus and his disciples. He would let Jesus know what the leaders said. Then Jesus would leave the area, and all would be fine.

The limestone rocks jutted out to the road, making obtuse figures as Steven and the lamb hurried on. Parts of the road seemed like a maze with walls zigzagging back and forth. They had just run through a particularly winding part of the path, and the road was opening up to the top of a hill when Steven saw them. Dogs!

They had definitely seen Steven and the lamb and were running and growling down the hill toward them. Steven turned to run but was boxed in by the limestone walls. Up was the only option. The commotion the dogs were making was getting louder. The lamb instinctively jumped on part of the wall and pawed his way up the side to safety. Steven tried to climb, but the lower edge of the wall offered no foothold for him to get started. Steven couldn't believe it. His whole life he had heard of the wild dogs, had only seen a glimpse of them a couple times while traveling with his father, and now they were right on top of him.

Suddenly, Steven felt himself being pushed. He looked to see that the lamb had jumped down and was pushing him up to get hold on the rocks. Steven got his footing and was scrambling up to a small ledge when he heard the dogs hit the lamb. There was no sound by the lamb, only the sound of six or seven dogs growling and fighting over their prize.

The world stopped. Steven screamed in terror and rage. He turned to jump down but was met face-to-face with a snarling dog. Steven could feel the dog's hot breath on his face and see sharp teeth and saliva as the dog snapped its jaws repeatedly with a force which would have surely broken a man's leg. He fell back against the side of the ledge and lay still. The dog could not make it up on the rock and soon joined the others.

With a rush of strength Steven had never experienced before, he began clawing his way up the hill away from the gruesome scene taking place below. There was no sound. No time.

Steven reached the top and pulled himself into the cool grass. He lay still for a moment, exhausted from the climb, and in his mind tried to manage what had just happened. The lurking danger became a realization again, and Steven was up. Across a small grassy field, Steven saw a small grove of trees and a group of men with several torches. Steven began running in that direction.

As he approached the group, he heard a man scream and hold the side of his head. He slowed and saw a man in the center of the group reach out to the injured man, and the screaming stopped. The men with torches grabbed this man, and all the other people in his group scattered.[21]

Steven stood still and could see it was Jesus they had seized. As the group with Jesus deserted, Steven was standing facing Jesus, who nodded his head as before, only without the smile. A look of great concern was on both their faces as the men bound Jesus and dragged him away.

"Steven? Is that you?" Steven finally realized it was his uncle Simon talking to him. "What are you doing out here? Are you by yourself? Come on. We've got to get out of here."

Steven's uncle was pulling his arm as Steven watched the group of men arresting Jesus. "Isn't there something we can do?" he asked softly.

"Not now," his uncle replied sharply. "I could have killed them all. They weren't expecting a fight. But that time has passed. Besides, I tried to rescue him, but he just helped them. Come on. We've got to get back to Jerusalem." Steven looked at his uncle, who pulled him away. Following at a distance, they walked to Jerusalem behind the mob that had arrested Jesus. Steven and his uncle waited outside the city to give the group they were following time to enter the city and clear the streets.

"I heard them say they were taking Jesus to the palace of the high priest. We should go there," his uncle said. There was no one in the streets. Steven saw only one guard at the gate who didn't even acknowledge them as they entered the city.

When Steven and his uncle arrived at the palace of the high priest, they stopped to warm themselves by a fire in the palace courtyard. "Now what?" Steven asked.

"I'm not sure," his uncle replied. "I should get you home. I need to get more help."

A girl who had been watching them from the palace walked closer. "You're one of his disciples," she said to Simon.

"No!" Simon replied. "I don't know what you're talking about."

Steven's uncle took him by the arm again and walked toward the entryway of the courtyard.

"Uncle Simon?" Steven asked in a concerned voice. "Why did you tell her you didn't know Jesus?"

"Listen, Steven," his uncle replied, "I wouldn't be helping anyone if I get arrested, too."

When they reached the gate another girl accused Simon again, "You were with him. You were with Jesus the Nazarene."

"You're crazy!" he denied. "I promise, I don't know the man."

Soon a group of others came to them. "We heard you," a man said. "Listen to you. You're a Galilean. Your accent gives you away. Surely you were with Jesus."

"Didn't I see you with him in the olive grove? Jesus called you Peter. You cut off my brother's ear!" another man in the group said.

More people were walking toward Steven and his uncle. "No, you fools! I wasn't with him!" Simon Peter emphatically denied.

At that moment, a rooster crowd in the distance. Simon stopped and became expressionless. Then he began to cry. He sobbed uncontrollably. The men who had been accusing him just stared. "Steven, go home," he managed to say and then ran away crying bitterly.[22]

Steven turned and walked slowly down the street away from the palace. He began to cry for the first time. He wasn't even aware it was his father who scooped him up in his arms and held him tight until he heard him speak. "Steven, you're safe. We've been so worried." Steven clung to his neck and sobbed as his father carried him. He was asleep by the time his father got back to May's house and laid him in bed.

CHAPTER TWENTY-FIVE

It was almost noon when Steven woke up. He lay still for quite some time thinking about everything that had happened the night before. He finally got up and walked to the front part of the house to find his mother and two aunts in the kitchen.

"Why is it dark outside?" Steven asked the ladies.

"We're not sure, Steven. Are you all right?" his mother asked as he sat down at the table. She pulled a chair close and sat with her arm around him as he told them what had happened on the road, then in the garden, and then at the palace. All three women wept as Steven told his story.

"I don't know why things happen the way they do sometimes," his mother finally said, wiping her eyes. "Your father said he heard the priest and leaders plan to crucify Jesus on a cross."

At this, Steven jumped from his chair. "Why?" he shouted. His aunts hung their heads, and his mother reached for him. "Why! How could this happen?" he yelled and ran back to his room, slamming the door.

Steven stayed in his room alone. His mother brought him something to eat and drink, but he wouldn't touch it. Later, Steven walked back to the front of the house and out the door into the dimly lit street without saying a word to anyone. He walked without thinking. He just walked. As he reached the upper part of the city, he saw Judi and his friends in the street. For a moment, Steven expected the worst, but Judi simply lowered his head and walked away.

Steven ended up at a place that overlooked the western hills outside the city. On the horizon was Golgotha. The small hill resembled a skull, and on its silhouette Steven could make out three crosses. A tear rolled down his cheek as he stood looking, and the sky mysteriously began to turn darker. Steven sat alone for quite some time. The last of the light disappeared, and Steven could no longer see anything out on the hills. Suddenly, Steven felt a tremor under his feet, and the earth began to shake. He braced himself against a post, and the shaking soon stopped. He started back home, making his way by torches that people had lit in the city as the sun sadly reappeared.[23]

The next morning Steven heard voices coming from the kitchen. He found his mother and father sitting at the table holding hands. "Steven," they said together. "How are you, partner?" his father asked as he hugged him close.

"Okay," he said quietly. "Are the stories true? Was that Jesus at Golgotha?" Steven asked.

"I'm afraid so," his father responded. "The news I heard was they crucified Jesus with two thieves. Messengers couldn't leave today because of the Sabbath, but we're to leave first thing in the morning for Capernaum with news of what has happened."

All Steven could do was shake his head. "Has anyone seen Uncle Simon?" Steven asked.

"No," said Steven's mother. "May is asking in town. Chloe is trying to find Andrew as well."

"I'm hungry," Steven said, looking to his mother who had already stood up.

"Yes. I'm sure you are," she said, placing a plate of fruit with some bread and fish and a cup of milk on the table in front of him.

Steven ate slowly and talked with his parents. No one mentioned the lamb.

After eating, Steven went back to his room. He lay down and fell asleep crying and didn't leave the house the entire day.

The next morning he rose early. His father was already loading their bags on the cart. "I'm glad you're up, Steven. They asked me to go by Galilee and deliver a message on our way back to Capernaum. Lots of ground to cover. We've got to get going."

"Goodbye, May." Steven's mother said as she hugged her sister. "We'll be back soon." She walked to the cart and Isa helped her into the seat. Steven pulled himself up over the wheel of the cart and got in the back. He waved to his aunt, who had a sad smile on her face as she waved back to him.

"We'll see you soon!" Isa yelled as he popped the reins, and the oxen began lumbering down the street ahead of the creaking cart.

Steven had nestled into the bags like he always did and watched the sky glow brighter and brighter as the sun rose.

The cart creaked rhythmically along, but Steven's mind was miles away.

They had ridden for hours when Steven's trance was broken by a horse and rider in the distance quickly approaching the cart from behind. Steven watched as the rider got closer, and he could make out more and more detail. The sound of the hooves became louder until it was definitely clear. The rider was his uncle Simon!

"Uncle Simon!" Steven shouted.

Both Steven's father and mother turned to see Simon race up beside them on a white horse and come to a bouncy stop.

"Simon!" Steven's mother exclaimed. "Where have you been, and what are you doing, and where did you get that horse?" she asked, too excited to sound scolding.

"He's alive!" Simon said. "John and I saw him. Mary and some of the other women saw him and talked to him!"

Steven was standing with his hands on his mother's shoulders. "Who, Simon? What are you talking about?" Isa asked.

"Jesus! He's alive!" Simon yelled, throwing his head back and laughing. "It's just like he said. 'Destroy this temple, and I will rebuild it in three days.' It wasn't the temple he was referring to. It was him, his body! He's alive!"

Simon was almost uncontrollable with excitement. The horse he was on pawed the ground, raised its head up and down vigorously as if agreeing with Simon, and then reared on its hind legs. Steven's mother turned and hugged him, and the three in the cart were overjoyed. "He told us to meet him at a mountain, here, near Galilee. We didn't know what he was talking about until now, but this is it."

Simon told Isa where the mountain was and then raced away as fast as the horse could carry him. "This is amazing," Steven's father said.

"Truly amazing," his mother agreed.

Steven's parents turned to him as he sat back down on the bags. "Well that's wonderful," Steven said. "But I guess I don't really have anything to ask Jesus now, do I?"

"Steven, this may be true," his father said wisely. "But we must look beyond ourselves."

"It is wonderful," Steven said with a heavy heart. He closed his eyes and rested as the cart slowly creaked along.

CHAPTER TWENTY-SIX

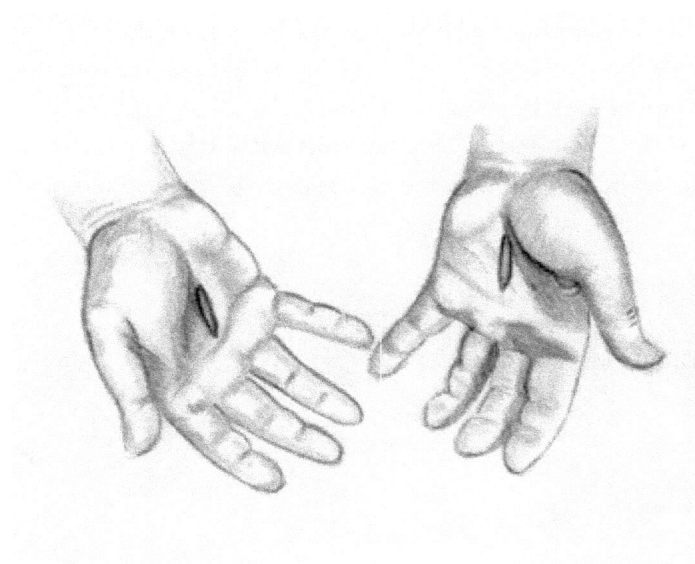

They had reached the small road Simon had told them to take that led up to a mountain. The small road soon became too rough for the cart, and Steven's father tied the oxen to a bush and gave them some water. "We'll walk from here. It can't be too much farther."

They walked up a short piece of trail that made a turn at the top and opened up into a level clearing on the side of the mountain. At the edge of the clearing, a man stood on a rock. He was facing a small group of people and had his back to Steven and his parents as they approached.

The man was definitely cradling something as he spoke to the group. "All authority in heaven and on earth has been given to me."

Steven listened closely as the man spoke. "Therefore go and make disciples of all nations, baptizing them in the name of the Father and of the Son and of the Holy Spirit. And teach them to obey everything I have commanded you."

As the man spoke, he began to turn, facing Steven and his parents. Then it was clear. It was Jesus. And what he was cradling in his arms was Steven's lamb. "And surely I am with you always, to the very end of the age," he continued as he knelt down and handed the lamb to Steven, smiling and nodding as he had done each time before.[24]

As Steven took the lamb, which immediately pressed his head next to Steven's face, marks were clearly visible in both of Jesus's open hands where they had been nailed to the cross.

"I've been wanting to talk to you," Jesus said to Steven.

"And me to you," Steven replied.

Jesus stepped down from the rock, and putting his hand on Steven's shoulder, he walked with Steven and the lamb.

THE LAMB

ENDNOTES

1 Matthew 5:44

2 John 5:1-18

3 John 2:12-22

4 John 3:26-30

5 Luke 3:19-20

6 Luke 5:1-11

7 Isaiah 53:3

8 Isaiah 53:5

9 John 1:29

10 Matthew 12:9-14

11 Mark 2:1-12

12 Luke 8:22-25

13 Mark 5:21-43

14 Matthew 14:1-12

15 John 6:1-15

16 Joshua 6:15-20

17 Luke 19:1-10

KEVIN ATCHLEY

THE LAMB